Dedication

To my brother, Jun…

who left too soon, but found an incredible way to say goodbye.

Rippling Waves

ANTHONY TERESI

A Spiritual Journey
Through the Heart of the Universe

Rippling Waves

ANTHONY TERESI

Tysargus Publishing

RIPPLING WAVES: A Spiritual Journey Through the Heart of the Universe

Copyright © 2021 by Anthony Teresi

All rights reserved. No portion of this book may be reproduced in any form without permission from the publisher, except as permitted by U.S. copyright law.

Tysargus Publishing

Editor: Jessica Bryan, www.oregoneditor.com
Creative Consultant and Technical Editor: Valentine Rose Bezar
Book Designer: Christy Collins, Constellation Book Services,
    www. constellationbookservices.com
Additional Photography: Allie Teresi

Illustrations:
"Age of Aquarius" © Pamela Matthews 1998 www.grail.co.nz
Illustration 197561734 © Alexandra Barbu | Dreamstime.com
Illustration 202884300 © Valery Rybakou | Dreamstime.com

ISBN (paperback): 978-1-7365326-0-7
ISBN (ebook): 978-1-7365326-1-4

Printed in the United States of America

PRAISE FOR RIPPLING WAVES

"A visionary book, written from the heart, wrapped in love, and delivered with the best of intentions: Anthony Teresi's *Rippling Waves* is a journey across a Universal bridge to enlightenment. Full of positivity and truth, this work will take you on a first-class guided soul's journey through time and space. So pour a cuppa, put on your cozy clothes, and settle down for a spiritual trip towards planetary unity."
—Dr. Penny March, author and Child and Family therapist

"Anthony Teresi's *Rippling Waves* is an incredible work that from the beginning shifts the reader into the luminosity of their being. From Chapter One on, the reader journeys with him into a new realm of being, stretching their perception to move ahead while focusing inward. When we reach this new world where ethereal artists create huge portraits of living light, the impact is stunning and inspirational. Celestial exaltation is revealed in Chapter Four and the reader is embraced by the divine revelation that Anthony has himself experienced.

I've known Anthony for many years and he has consistently shown that he is ahead of his time as an adept and compassionate mystic. This book is not only personal, it is also revelatory and expansive. I invite you to read this celebration of human spirituality, and enjoy the rippling waves of possibility."
—Shan Watters, author of *Earthstaria, Mothering the Divine* and *The Rainbow Wind*

"In his book, *Rippling Waves: A Spiritual Journey through the Heart of the Universe,* Anthony stirs the emotions and presents a visual storyboard that is a banquet fit for any spiritual seeker. We are encouraged to go within, get a clear vision, step forward and allow ourselves to enter a new world, leaving fear and resistance behind. Are you ready to take the journey?"

—Patricia Cooley

"As I read these words I am reminded of why awareness and growth are so important on my spiritual journey. These places represented within the passages are the goal for so many of us. I'm drawn in to the landscapes and the places, the beings that inhabit them, the sights, sounds, and energy that is felt. Reading on I see the potentiality of working hard on my own spirituality and attaining the levels of enlightenment that are detailed within this work. Knowing that I am not alone on this journey and knowing that others will be there in thought and consciousness to become one in flowing harmony is an inspiration.

I fully support and endorse this incredible work. I look forward to opening myself and traveling the path that Rippling Waves offers to all seekers of spiritual attainment."

—Michael Vukich

"This extraordinary work, *Rippling Waves*, reveals a spiritual journey that is rarely experienced and shared with others. For those people who have never experienced such amazing connections with the spiritual world, may you live your life in such a way that these portals begin to open to you. Many have tried to artificially stimulate such experiences through various techniques and/or the use mind-altering substances. They are often called Seekers. Here is the true story of the spiritual journey from one who has the courage to share — Anthony Teresi. We are all the richer for having known this wise loving man."

—Barbara Wilson

ACKNOWLEDGEMENTS

Special thanks and much gratitude to:

Valentine Rose Bezar, for her invaluable editing, technical and creative contributions. Her steadfast belief and unwavering commitment in seeing this book through to its conclusion have contributed greatly to the finished quality of this work.

Christy Collins and Constellation Book Services for her superb design and team of highest quality professionals who complemented every aspect of this work.

Martha Bullen at Bullen Publishing Services, for her intelligent guidance and excellent advice, marketing insight, and technical expertise.

Jessica Bryan, for editing, initial encouragement and references to pertinent industry resources.

Shan Watters, Penny March, Barbara Wilson, Patricia Cooley, Michael Vukich for your stellar recommendations.

CONTENTS

Terms and Concepts   *xvii*
Prologue   *xxiii*
Introduction   1
How I Got From There to Here   5
Note to the Reader   17

Chapter One: THE WAY REVEALED   **19**
TRANSFORMATIONAL CONSCIOUSNESS

Solo Flight   21
The Maiden and the Bedouin   22
The Man in the Copper Dish   33
Meeting My Messengers   36
The Priestess   42
The Jewel   46
The Choice   49
Destiny's Realization   52

Chapter Two: BEING ALL   **55**
TRANSCENDENT CONSCIOUSNESS

Prelude   57
The Journey   58
Trasara!   59
Our Guide   60
The Globes   63
The Lovers   68
The Mores   70
Ethereal Artists   71
The Gift   78
The Opalescent Seas of Trasara   80

Those Beyond	84
Reflections	85
Magnificence Awaits	87

Chapter Three: UNIVERSE OF UNIVERSES — 91
COSMIC CONSCIOUSNESS

Higher and Deeper	93
The Mighty Angel	102
The Milky Way and Beyond	104
The Fountain	107
Who Is Looking?	111
Is There No End?	116
Spirit Daughter	117
Scenes of Creation	120
The Invisible Center	121
Beyond Ideas—The Secret of Creation— The Pyramid of Presence	124
Presence: The Child of Three	127
From the Greatest to the Least	129

Chapter Four: SOURCE — 135
DIVINE CONSCIOUSNESS

Prelude	137
BLACKNESS	138
The Fall	142
The Garden of Lilac	147
On The Threshold	148
The Mandorla	149
The Dove	151
The Imaginal	155
The Flute	157
Our Own Lives	169
The Return	175

Chapter Five: UNITY   **183**
UNITY CONSCIOUSNESS

Trasara Revisited	185
The Tale	186
The Old Ruling Order	188
Renaissance	194
The Vanguard	195
The Law of Emergence	200
Barriers	202
Baby Steps	204
The Search	205
The Leap	210
The Old Awakens	213
Victory	219
The New Dawn	222
The Planet Glows	224
The Shift	226
Contact	230
Homecoming	233
Return to the Moment	236
Final Words	238
A Global Love Affair	*245*

TERMS AND CONCEPTS

As you embark on this journey, you will repeatedly come upon important touchstone terms. These words or phrases embody ever-expanding, limitless concepts and meanings.

In an attempt to define the indefinable, I am sharing merely a few of these universal meanings.

In truth, these inspiring word concepts are universal in nature.

SOURCE:

God, Creator, I AM
The Alpha and Omega
The Transcendent Reality
The Highest Deity of Any and All Religions, Philosophies, Theologies or Concepts
The Ultimate Being
God The Father
Brahma... and Beyond

CONSCIOUSNESS:

God The Son
God The Mother
Awareness

The Logos
The Word
Cosmic Mother
The Goddess
The Creative Principle
Breath of Life, All Motion and Reality
Everything Knowable and Unknowable
Vishnu... and Beyond

PRESENCE / THE PRESENCE PRINCIPLE:

The Holy Spirit
The Fabric of Reality
The Field
That Within Which Form Appears
Maya
Light
Dark Energy
Dark Matter
God The Spirit
Shiva... and Beyond

ESSENCE:

Our Spirit
Our Soul
Our Personal Identity
Our Life
Spiritually, Everything We Are

The Co-Creator
The Atman... and Beyond

EMANATION:

Gravity
An abstract but perceptible vibration
A radiance that issues forth or originates from Source
The moving force whereby frequency is initiated
The Creative Act in motion
The Action of Being
The Aura... and Beyond

ADDITIONAL TERMS

FREQUENCY

The rate at which a *vibration* occurs creates a *wave*, either in a material (as in sound waves) or in an electromagnetic field (as in radio waves and light). Frequencies, usually measured per second, occur throughout the entire spectrum of reality—physical, emotional, mental, and spiritual—and extend far beyond our limited perceptions. *Frequencies* are used to determine and differentiate *vibrational patterns*. These patterns or forms are expressed as waves of the finest individuation bringing identity to each thing, from particles to galaxies. The words *vibrational frequencies* are often used together, and along with the force of gravity they are the generators of all mass.

TORUS FIELD (Part 3)

An electromagnetic frequency that arcs out from the heart, and back again. It is referred to as a *Torus Field*. This is believed to be the oldest structure in existence. Its shape is similar to that of a donut. The motion of its energy continually folds in a circular pattern, constantly and perpetually refreshing itself. Typically, this is an aspect of light as it is seen around angels and celestials.

MANDORLA (Part 4)

The *Mandorla* is the intersection, where soul and spirit meet. It also represents the common field of interaction between different dimensions and the expression of soul. The Mandorla is an ancient symbol of two circles coming together, overlapping one another to form an almond shape in the middle. It is also known as the *Vesica Piscis* within The Flower of Life cosmology, which is another symbol that expresses growth by division.

GEO-CENTERS AND CENTRES (Part 5)

Geo-centers are natural locations where magnetism from the core of the planet fuses with electricity of the atmosphere giving rise to the electromagnetic spark of life. These are areas where stabilizing lifeforce energy continually emerges and interacts to perpetually nourish all existence. Known as Mother Nature's power points, they have been used by many cultures for millennia past.

Centre is the term used to describe the human made sites physically erected or constructed at or near the geo-centers for the purpose of tuning into and harnessing these natural forces for the betterment and facilitation of global unity. Each Centre is unique to the site energy it has been constructed on and is built to express that particular geo-energy.

PROLOGUE

R*ippling Waves: A Spiritual Journey Through the Heart of the Universe,* has been created for those who wish to transcend the day-to-day routines of life and embrace a greater vision of love and inspiration. While it may not seem so on the surface, there is a quiet yet powerful movement emerging in the world that seeks unity, peace and a deep soul healing. This book's message, which speaks to the value of awareness expansion, will challenge many of the current social, ethical and spiritual norms of the day.

A well-known author recently conducted an experiment connecting women around the globe via video chat. They all came from different cultures that for generations had been taught to hate and fear *those* people. When the screens flashed on and each one could see the other, face to face, they discovered that they all shared the same hopes and dreams. Each one desired a safe home, an end to war, and the freedom and opportunity to provide life's necessities and abundance for themselves and their families. These are *human qualities* we all share. They realized that the perpetuated false beliefs of fear and hatred had built up the walls of separation keeping them from working together to achieve their common goals. It also became clear that this separation was the key that allowed those in power to continue breeding the paradigm of distrust of "the other." As long as we allow those with an agenda of greed to spin their fantasy of fear and hatred, they will continue to succeed in blinding us from the truth that connects all humankind.

Rippling Waves puts forward a different set of values, and calls for a renaissance of spiritual and planetary harmony. We must first however, as individuals, achieve an elevated perception of awareness before realizing the promise of an expanded global unity. A shift in our personal and collective consciousness must come to be. The pathway to uplifted awareness and attainment of higher wisdom has been kept hidden from the masses and revealed through but a relatively few spiritual teachings and masters. In truth, these innate gifts are part of our human design and have always been there, calling out, urging us to develop and grow. The very definition of the experience of transformation into expanded awareness has almost been lost, yet when we stop and realize the truth that all human beings are one and the same, the path to enlightenment opens magnificently before us.

This journey through the heart of the universe speaks to our greatest self, and in offering a divine opportunity to look upward *and* inward, we realize that love is the greatest power. Perhaps this sounds naive or even like a Pollyanna, given our state of current affairs. It is, however not only the truth, but indeed the *greatest* truth.

Rippling Waves offers much more than the mere concept of passing into a new age. These ideas represent the very truth of life itself! This journey clearly shows that until the majority of us awaken and seize the waiting gauntlet of the heart, our world will continue to crash and burn, survive, rebuild, then crash again and again as the promise of universal peace and oneness continues to pass us by. It does not have to be this way. Life *can* transform and humanity *can* facilitate that transformation.

We see old school mystics who have guarded their secrets for millennia, coming together with the new school of science philosophers, forging a deep bond dedicated to discovering new solutions and a new vision for the upliftment of our entire planet. In the spirit of an unshakable certainty that all life has supreme value, amazing things are happening to facilitate the expansion of human consciousness. I invite you to experience this book and ride the *Rippling Waves* with an open heart, that we may all find our own way through the maze into this new day together. I guarantee you it IS there, waiting for all of us.

INTRODUCTION

Imagine for a moment the simplicity of a pebble and a pond.... If we drop a pebble into a still pond, we create rippling waves. If we continue to drop pebbles into the pond, we can sustain the ripples and the waves.

Expanding this vision into life itself, we liken the continuing drop of the pebble to each beat of our heart, and depict the pond as the boundless ocean of consciousness within which all Creation exists. In this comparison, like the pebble, it is the continuing pulse of our beating heart that sustains our life. Our awareness emerges and like the waves rippling out, it expands across the infinite ocean of consciousness.

At the very first instant of our creation, we become a divine vibration. Our birth is an expression of our individual "Now," because the first pulse of our heart creates the waves that expand from this point of emergence. One of the greatest mysteries is that, while there seems to be a definitive acceptance of our physical existence, it is not always with the same sense of certainty that the *totality* of our identity is known. While it is possible to see the waves of our consciousness, this might never happen until a way to rise above the most basic sense of the illusion of self is found.

The ripples or dimensions of our lives can be felt or

perceived only when we connect to the greater intelligence within us. After gaining the ability to rise above the all-encompassing roar of our present, we begin to see a greater reality. Once attained, each rippling wave flowing from our center represents the multidimensional quality of our life, expanding out into eternity.

The beating of our heart is the continuous action that moves the waves outward and inward. These pulsations become our authentic signature of life as they radiate into the unknown regions of all. No one can perceive or completely know the inexplicable universe. Yet, even though only the boundaries of our physical bodies can be seen, we must always strive, through our personal and collective courage to grow beyond the limitations of these perceptions. Although we cannot know everything, we can always know more.

Taking a broader view can reveal an even grander panorama. Each one of the many lives existing in the entire universe vibrates within this perpetual living expression of all creation. Our observations show that each life creates its own rippling waves, and these waves intersect and overlap with the life waves of every other living being. Crisscrossing and impacting one another, the rippling waves of each life intermingle and interact with all other lives within the same sea of infinite consciousness. This is a simple metaphor that illustrates the true reality of all creations in the cosmos.

The nature of multidimensional existence is one

of the great mysteries we will explore together as we create and expand our awareness of consciousness.

Rippling Waves: A Spiritual Journey Through the Heart of the Universe represents the living, ever-radiating heart of Source that brings life to all. Knowable only through love, Source has expressed consciousness as the sea within which everything is in a perpetual state of *coming to be.* Through the highest expression of creativity and love, we can come to know Oneness with this unfathomable expression.

It is these profound insights of wisdom that we seek to reveal. Perhaps your own prescient knowing will see these realities as they unfold, or it might be your spirit's imagination that comes alive and vibrant. Tapping into the intuitive and mystical gifts that are possessed by all, we will journey on, expanding into our greatest realities.

The states of consciousness we will be visiting are: transformational, transcendent, cosmic, divine, and unity. These states, or *perceptions of being,* are known by countless names, and there are others we could have used. However, it is not their designations we seek, but rather their experience.

Each person reading this will recognize these states and understand according to his or her own desires and abilities. To illustrate, consider the make-up of a choir, specifically the soprano and the bass voices. Both sing in the choir. However, these voices represent very different sounds by which they are able to vibrate their own unique qualities and frequencies. The unique tone and vibration of each voice resonates within the total choir, reflecting their ultimate identity. The voices are to the heartbeat what the choir is to the sea of consciousness. Each of us, according to our own personal talents and abilities, is singing in the universal choir!

Imagine, as well, that each insight we encounter along our way is like a pearl on a string that spirals higher and higher. Each pearl is beautiful in and of itself, and if we listen closely it will tell us the divine story of its very creation. Yet, ultimately, it is the string, that unseen *Presence* connecting the pearls, that creates a necklace of even greater glory. In this way, each pearl participates beyond its own limitations, becoming part of and enhancing the greater beauty of the whole. *Rippling Waves: A Spiritual Journey Through the Heart of the Universe* is such a necklace, aspiring to express the greatest revelations of love and multidimensional living.

Exploring these states of awareness will become the heart and soul of our journey as we reach out to fully grasp and embrace our true nature. We are more than just bodies existing in the illusion of space and time. We are the heartbeat of love bursting forth into life, casting itself over and over again upon the ocean of consciousness, reaching ever onward toward Source. Come, let us begin....

HOW I GOT FROM THERE TO HERE

If I had to narrow down my individual journey, it would come from asking myself, in one way or another, these deeply profound questions. Perhaps they will sound familiar to you, because they are the same questions humanity has been asking since the beginning of time:

Who am I? Why am I here? What is my purpose? What is the true nature of my reality?

I can say beyond all doubt that I have questioned the nature of my own, as well as any and all realities I've encountered, over and over again. In order to examine anything, however, I have found that I must first seek to know *who* I am. It is only through "knowing that I know" that I can question anything at all. How can I question a particular reality if I am not aware of its existence? It is the very nature of this ever-expanding awareness that continually inspires me to seek, to learn, and to grow to the greatest measure possible.

Do I know with absolute certainty *where* I am?

If I ask myself where I am, I can simply say that I am here, standing right here. But, where is here?

Is *here* my body, my mind, the planet, this day, this instant, this solar system, galaxy, or universe? Where exactly is *here*? What was once thought to be a simple question turns out to be quite profound, because in order to identify *where I am,* I must first discover *who I am,* and *why I exist.*

Pursuing the answers to these questions will bring us an ocean of new awareness flooding in. This is where we will begin.

But first, let us return to consider an earlier time of first beginnings.

I began asking questions about consciousness many years ago. I have had countless opportunities throughout the course of my life to pursue in-depth and profound understanding, and I have had the good fortune to travel in multiple directions searching for answers.

I have been blessed with natural abilities and boundless curiosity. These qualities have always been the driving force that spurred me onward to knowing what's beyond the next bend, around the next corner, or over the next mountain. Originally, I began to pursue the vast mystery of personal consciousness expansion without even knowing I was doing it. I always felt there was more to life… more to see, more to learn, and more to know.

I started out as a musician, metaphysician, and astrologer. Through these three major paths I was able to pursue the nature of awareness from the intellectual and creative points of view, as well as the intuitive and spiritual.

I have observed many disciples who dedicated their entire lives to pursuing these very same aspirations. In a precious few, the levels of attainment were unprecedented and beautiful. Too often, though, these seekers became disillusioned. They had committed their lives to dogmatic or traditional ways of attainment, achieving what seemed to be temporary and unfulfilling results holding only disappointment. Personally, I have found enlightenment to be a journey that cannot be taught. It can only be revealed through inner growth. Transformation can only happen with true commitment to discovery of the Divine Light within.

For me, curiosity does not always lend itself to patience. In a hurry to know, I was not inclined to pursue a course of steadfast commitment and dedication, early on. Thus, in an attempt to take the fast track to enlightenment, I engaged in early experimentation with mind expansive substances. I tried them all.

Revolutionary and fascinating, this period of my life introduced me to the fact that there are realities beyond the mere three-dimensional. Through these experiences, I was transported to many different states of awareness, not really knowing where I was, only to witness for what seemed like a moment the fact that a far greater reality actually existed. I would then be thrust back into the same everyday life I had just left, perhaps only a few short hours earlier. While these observations were fruitful, unfortunately they did not grant me the true mastery I was seeking. As mentioned, while this path was productive, after a period of time it was no longer fulfilling. Shortcuts along the way never supplied the desired result of owning awareness of the greater realities I was seeking. I learned the hard lesson that when it comes to achieving expanded awareness and an ultimate relationship with consciousness, there simply are—and can be—no shortcuts.

As time went on, with the exception of my family life, I spent most of my waking hours pursuing the mastery of musical expression as a creative art form. In order to accomplish this, I had to embrace what turned out to be a complete spiritual, emotional, mental, and physical commitment. Fortunately, in addition to these primary artistic pursuits, I had already been practicing yoga for many years.

Yoga was the very best of disciplines necessary to achieve the ability of mastering the deep inner focus needed to perfect the art of performance. It was the best possible method for helping me stay centered.

Being able to step aside from the all-encompassing awareness of my body to facilitate the perfection of creative expression was very difficult. It took a continuing and ongoing expansion of conscious awareness to achieve this ability. This is not an unusual statement and, certainly, many master musicians and artists have made similar observations about their own achievements, *especially when it comes to being truly in the moment of performance.* Achieved through sheer dedication and commitment to the highest goal of consummate inspired mastery, I was able to gain, in the truest sense of the word, a degree of fluency and wisdom far beyond my early beginnings.

All through these times, I was also having mystical experiences, but I wasn't aware they were, indeed, clairvoyant visions. *I have seen things since I was a child, and have often known about events before they happened.* This was a common occurrence within my family circle, so I never really thought much of it. Not until later in life did I realize that, although we all have these abilities within us, not everyone possesses the awareness or ability to tune into them.

During this period, I had an intense, even voracious desire to learn. I absorbed a massive amount of information and knowledge in the study of many works, from Eastern and Western Philosophy to Mysticism, Theosophy, Ontology, and Cosmology. I also explored the most profound works of many masters and sages, and their wisest teachings, cultures, and belief systems, past, present, and what has turned out to be future. As I saw these paths inevitably converge and merge, I began to see clearly the universal correlation that exists in so much of what is considered diverse. It wasn't until I had my first true spiritual encounter, however, that I realized the actuality of other dimensions.

I will explain…

Due to a family emergency, I found myself in the

jungles of Mexico pursuing the unexpected disappearance of my brother, whose plane had vanished during a storm. He was on the radar preparing to land in Acapulco, when suddenly his plane was gone, lost somewhere between Ixtapa and Acapulco.

My family was devastated. I traveled from Los Angeles to Mexico desperate for answers. I covered every road, every village, and every trail in that wildly remote area. I hired guides to take me up into the mountains and as far as the jungle would allow. I spoke to as many people as I could, hoping that someone had seen or heard something, anything, but it was all to no avail. After two weeks, having exhausted every possibility, I had to face the fact that no one knew anything about my brother's whereabouts. The situation seemed hopeless and I felt quite helpless and sad. When I originally left for Mexico, I felt confidant. I believed I would find him, one way or another. Now, I had to return home and tell my family that my search had been unsuccessful.

As I sat in my hotel room with tears welling up in my eyes, pondering these tragic events, a sublime sensation of peace came over me. *In this deepest moment of despair, my brother appeared in front of me.*

All of a sudden, I could see him, actually see him. He looked just as he always had in our youth. He was smiling and optimistic, and he seemed prepared to move on to a future I could not see. Indescribable shock, joy, and love radiated through me, all at once. As we spoke, he told me that his plane had crashed in the mountains and would most likely never be found. Before he left to take the next step of his journey, he wanted to be sure that I knew he had "made it." He was moving on, to where I didn't know, but he was visibly thrilled. He had waited for my arrival to say goodbye, and he wanted me to tell everyone he was sorry he had to leave and that he loved them. Then he vanished!

How can I express the feelings that went through me in that precious moment? By many standards his appearance was impossible. Yet there it was, a full-blown new reality. *My first transcendent experience had just unfolded right before my eyes.* It was definitely my brother and we did have that conversation, just as I have described. In that timeless instant, another dimension was revealed to me, along with the realization that the fabric of reality is far more than what our sensibilities tell us. I had seen and spoken with my brother, who was on the *other side*, but I was not using my physical senses. My body began to shake, as tears of both sorrow and happiness streamed down my face. It was the most precious of moments, like nothing I had ever known. I would not realize it until a few years later, but my entire life had been shifted and transformed into a new perception of reality. Saying goodbye to my brother before he had fully passed over was the greatest gift of all.

When I returned home, I told my family about the extraordinary encounter I shared with him. Of course, there were many mixed emotions and reactions. But because of the mysterious disappearance of the plane and the fact he was never found, it was still difficult to fully accept that he was gone. Still hoping against all hope, my mother began to seek out psychics who said they could help. Thus began our journey into the world of psychic phenomenon, divination, and the associated mystical arts.

Five years later, we received a report from the Mexican government stating that, quite accidentally, the wreckage of my brother's plane had finally been found on the side of a mountain some 8,000 feet above sea level. It was located on a dense hillside covered with trees that would have been impossible to find or even reach. It was then that I realized the true reason I had been drawn to Mexico was to have this miraculous personal breakthrough, showing me that love is infinite, existing beyond all boundaries of space and time.

As life went on, I discovered my awareness had changed. I began seeing imagery that was somewhat similar to what I had been shown in my earlier days. Back then I was able to see through the use of mind-expanding substances; yet now, *I could see without inducements of any kind.* Defying explanation, I began seeing auras around people, along with rare displays of remarkable color and light. Because of my transcendent experience in Mexico, I was able to witness and embrace my newly-awakened abilities with fearless certainty.

Everything changed. I noticed a higher awareness

and deeper consciousness emerging. This greatly enhanced my expression of music and elevated my understanding and grasp of what I was studying in the metaphysical realms. In addition, my psychic abilities continued to evolve and grow stronger, until I finally understood and accepted the truth of who I am.

After this breakthrough, I discovered I was able to communicate quite easily with Beings from the celestial realms and other realities. As my evolution continued, I began to see the many different dimensions in which we exist. I realized how the subtle vibrational difference between each frequency determines the nature of Creation's countless realms.

My awareness expanded exponentially and life itself began to take on a deeper meaning. As a musician and composer, I was inspired to create new, one-of-a-kind instruments. These instruments were vibrational in nature, designed to affect the body by resonating in ways that tuned into each person according to their individual frequency. In this fashion, I found that I was able to assist in many healings and enhance techniques of deeper meditation. My mind filled with wondrous ideas and new ways of approaching music beyond the traditional twelve-tone scale that is so commonly used today. I found myself being invited into many different ensembles, in which my soul-inspired instruments were featured and the audience reception was exhilarating. Powerful healings and spiritual awakenings took place during these vibrational performances, deeply affecting me and bringing great wellbeing to all who were present.

As my clairvoyant abilities began to grow, I focused on how to navigate the new path my waking spirit was creating. At first, I was unsure how I could implement these newly emerging talents. I began offering complimentary readings, utilizing a variety of my natural gifts of intuition and clairvoyance, along with the techniques of astrology and oracle interpretation.

Initially, I went through the inner conflict that so many in this field face. Ethically and morally it was imperative to know that what I was seeing was actually the past, present, and future, and not merely the meanderings of an over-active imagination. At this point, I began to transition away from music and stepped into the realm of fully embracing my gifts as a psychic and clairvoyant. I just *knew* it was the next evolutionary stage of my life. Much to my delight, the response was overwhelmingly positive. *In reading after reading, I saw images of how the events in people's lives had occurred.* As their continuing process of unfoldment passed before me, and from the reciprocal comments I was receiving, I realized that what I was seeing was real and not just my imagination. Taking this path showed me how I could help humanity in a more intimate and connected way, and led me to a greater spiritual understanding of myself and the phenomena of the universe.

Time progressed, and as I was drawn to even more profound studies, I found myself revisiting certain works that had escaped my understanding when I first discovered them. Initially, the true nature and meaning of these texts and insights had eluded me. Yet now, I found my vision had become illuminated and the deeper significance was crystal clear. Further and further, I delved into the most esoteric works and teachings available. I realized I was no longer just reading words on a page, because the words themselves began to spring to life and turn into vivid imagery. These sights and feelings filled me with wonder and instilled a driving passion that became the reality of my new inspiration.

I mention these developments now, prior to the stories that follow, so you will understand the journey I've taken and why I've decided to write this book. At this time in history, even more than centuries past, the entire world is asking and seeking answers to the eternal questions of life. I do not profess to know all the truths or all of life's secrets, but I do believe this journey into consciousness can help each of us reach a deeper understanding of *who* we are, *where* we are, *what* we are, and *why* we are here.

It is my privilege to offer but a whisper of the countless possibilities that exist for all humankind. My hope, too, is that *Rippling Waves* will bring some degree of clarity to the awakening souls who for so long have sought deeper ways of understanding their own unique experiences. It is with the pure intention of inspiring all humanity to grow into the greatest enlightenment of their soul-felt desires that I humbly present to you this journey through consciousness.

May *Rippling Waves* open hearts and minds, illuminating the way along our collective path. May this re-awakening lead us to the truth and the gift of knowing our own divine creation and each soul's special place in this eternal moment of Now. May it be a shining source of inspiration in remembering who we really are.

Each of us is a gift of love from the Heart of Source.

NOTE TO THE READER

To be clear, what follows in the stories ahead are my own spiritual experiences. They are not "made up," nor are they the imaginings of fiction. There have been some encounters, however, that have been so abstract or beyond measure as to defy direct description. I have attempted to express these visions as closely as possible to the original interactions using elevated language and metaphor.

These revelations are the reflections of many singular and multiple experiences that have come to me over a lifetime. Some fall into the category of synesthesia, while others reflect a bonding communion with higher dimensions and the life that exists therein. I have woven them into one story to give them structure and perspective.

Everything you will read on the pages that follow flows from a reality that has expressed itself at some point in and through me. To some these events may seem fantastical, but they are not. These experiences are available to all who would seek such spiritual adventures, and it is in the spirit of that reality that I share them with you now.

TRANSFORMATIONAL CONSCIOUSNESS

Chapter One

THE WAY REVEALED

SOLO FLIGHT

Out of light streams bursting forth from within the center of my consciousness, there appeared a beautiful iridescent field of pure energy through which the most radiant and loving face of a woman shone through. A brilliant golden hue surrounded her, and in a flash, a beam of light connected our hearts. No words were spoken, but there was the most extraordinary sense of having known her before. Although I had no idea who she was or where she had come from, I instantly felt we were One. Through her eyes the wisdom of the ages shone clear and bright. As the energy between our hearts became brighter, a mysterious tale began to unfold that, at first, seemed to be about someone else. It was not until its conclusion that I realized whose story it was... and the real reason for her coming.

THE MAIDEN AND THE BEDOUIN

Once there was a pretty young maiden who would rise each morning to go about her daily tasks. Looking through the window, she would see the same ordinary surroundings leading out to the distant horizon. This view changed very little over time, yet she never really gave it much thought. As she went about her regular duties, each day was the same as the day before, and everything fell into a similar predictable pattern. She had not chosen this lifestyle, yet this was the situation she found herself in. Looking around her world, she observed many other individuals in similar circumstances. Occasionally, she wondered with casual curiosity why so many others lived such ordinary, uneventful lives, but not much attention was ever really paid to it.

One morning, upon awakening to go about her daily routine, she looked out of the window and realized something seemed different. All of the usual landscapes and people she was so familiar with were still there, yet in some curious way it looked like the horizon had *moved* slightly closer to her. This continued to happen for a few days, and as each morning arrived she noticed *the distance between her home and the horizon was actually diminishing*. It became quite disconcerting trying to understand why this was happening. As she attended to her everyday activities, opportunities would arise to ask her friends, "Do you see, or have you noticed that each day the horizon seems to be moving closer?" No one could answer, or the ones who did said they had not noticed. Because no one else saw this, her fear began to grow. She felt so alone with her changing vision.

Without explanation, each day the horizon continued to appear closer and closer. So much so, that soon it felt like her life was taking place on a large island. Each morning she became more and more frantic, until she rushed out and exclaimed, "Do you see it, do you see it? Help! The horizon is closing in on us!" But, to her dismay, no one believed her, and her pleas were ignored. She had no way of knowing if what she was seeing was real or only her imagination.

Feeling like the world was closing in on her, her sense of extreme anxiety and fear were overwhelming. Filled with frustration and apprehension, she began to question her own sanity. But then, one day, it happened. *The horizon arrived at her very doorstep.* Frightened out of her wits, she just sat and stared out of her window, finally falling asleep to sobs that no one could hear.

When she woke up the next day, she ran to her window and was overjoyed to discover that the view was now as it should be. The horizon was once again at a great distance. Believing her sanity had been restored, she breathed a sigh of relief and gave thanks. Unfortunately, these feelings were short-lived, because just as her fear was lifting she looked closer and could not believe her eyes! The unthinkable had occurred. The houses, the stores, the streets, the people, everything she had come to know as reality, had simply vanished! Shocked and dismayed, each direction she turned showed only unending desert sands where her world once stood. Now she could only see a desert that extended out to the distant horizon, far beyond view. What impossible circumstance could have happened to account for this? It was not a dream. Her life and all that she had known had truly vanished.

Alone in the desert with no indication of direction, or why the life that she had come to rely on was apparently gone, her eyes lifted to the heavens searching for some sign or answer. Wherever she looked for something that held meaning, there was only endless desert and complete disappointment.

Suddenly there appeared a single Bedouin, sitting high atop a camel on a sand dune, smiling at her. She ran to meet him, begging him to help her understand what was happening. He spoke, but she could not understand what he was saying. Frustrated, at her wit's end and having become very thirsty, she motioned to the Bedouin that it was water she sought. He understood and pointed toward the horizon. She turned and began walking into the unknown desert, seeking some sort of understanding as to why this was happening. But now, more importantly, her need was simple... how would she satisfy her overwhelming thirst?

After walking many hours, just as she was about to give up from thirst and exhaustion, there appeared in the distance a shimmering image of loveliness with palm trees and blue waters. The image offered hope in her desert of nothing. Faster and faster she ran toward the horizon with optimism and anticipation, but when she arrived her hope turned to despair. Sadly, the vision of the oasis was only an illusion that had evaporated into nothingness. What looked to be palm trees, flowing waters, and beautiful voices beckoning her was, in fact, only sand, just more empty sand. She sat and wept in despair. Her sorrow and disappointment were numbing and complete.

As the days, weeks, and months passed, the same endless cycle happened over and again. She would see the shimmering oasis on the horizon and immediately run toward it, hoping that this time, maybe this time, it would be real. Desperately, she longed to dive into the cool waters and replenish her waning spirit. But alas, each vision turned out to be yet another mirage. Hope melted before her eyes and disappeared, revealing once again that it was nothing but sand and only more emptiness.

Always feeling like she was at the edge of her endurance, years passed as she encountered illusion after illusion, aimlessly wandering through the never-ending desert. Disappointment, despair, and anger were her constant companions, with the exception of the Bedouin on the camel, who occasionally appeared and tried to speak with her. He offered to teach her his language so they could communicate. Perhaps then, he could better designate where and in what direction would be most beneficial to find what she was seeking. But in her frustration, she refused to believe his attempts could help. In her mind, he was only a Bedouin! How could he possibly comprehend her plight? Even trying to talk with him seemed like a waste of time. She had but one singular pursuit, and her only objective was to find the oasis.

As the decades passed, it became obvious that she was a maiden no longer. Having grown old, her beauty had faded, as the harsh and unforgiving sands had taken their toll, and the lack of true nourishment had robbed her of youth and vitality. Her hair had turned gray and was laden thick with sand. Her body was wrinkled and aged from the unrelenting sun. With no sandals, her clothes tattered and worn, she walked endlessly over the burning sands. This is what she endured every day until she could face it no longer.

In her wanderings, she had discovered an ominous place: a cliff high above a bottomless abyss. She would go there when her sorrows were unbearable. There, the temptation to fling herself into the abyss and end her living nightmare forever was always present. But deep down, she knew that if she made this choice, the oasis would never be found and there would surely be no return from the bottomless chasm. The only solution was to continue her search in hope of reaching what was still her heart's fervent desire.

As she sat contemplating her fate, lamenting her wrinkled hands, she looked up and there, once again, was the Bedouin, radiating a peaceful and beautiful smile. Somehow, he just seemed to know the depth of her despair and discouragement at never finding the oasis. Finally, she began to appreciate that since he apparently lived in this place, maybe he knew more than she originally presumed. Perhaps, in fact, he might be her only hope.

Approaching him, she tried to communicate that she was finally ready, indeed willing to learn his language. At this point, after years of discounting his ability to help, it began to occur to her that through him, a way to the true oasis might be found.

The Bedouin began teaching her slowly but surely, and as her comprehension of his language grew, she came to see why she had been chasing dancing deceptions. He explained the mirages were only fantasies, merely illusions representing what she was really seeking. For without consciously knowing it, lying dormant and unexpressed within her, there was an unquenchable thirst to know love in the highest measure.

Because of the monotonous drone-like existence of her former life, her unknown desire had been buried within, with no space to flower. Beginning to surface now, from the depth of her heart, was the extraordinary realization that this had always been her truth. At last, she could see why her old unfulfilled life had vanished.

Her love simply *could not* be extinguished. In crying out, it rose up to manifest itself as the desire for an Oasis of Eternal Flowing Waters.

Her innermost truth had suddenly become crystal clear. Unseen and deep within her, refusing to surrender, the strength and power of love itself had literally designed and created the life conditions needed to actualize its own discovery. She realized that her search in the desert had only been with her eyes, not with her heart. Connecting with the Bedouin and receiving his wisdom and knowledge was the key that would ultimately help her find her way.

Through the profound insights gleaned from the lessons of the Bedouin's teachings, a different kind of vision began to appear on the horizon. Although it looked like just another illusion, she felt there was something different about it. An emotional tide deep within her began to stir. Daring to hope this might be her moment of truth, when she would at last fulfill her undeniable yearning to know, she began moving toward it.

With each breath, each step, and every beat of her heart, her anticipation grew. She walked on slowly and deliberately, drawing closer to the image on the horizon. But this time the vision wasn't fading away. It was becoming clearer, brighter, and more beautiful with each passing moment.

Finally reaching the edge where the dry desert met the lush green meadow, she saw it was indeed the oasis her heart had been seeking for so long. Cautiously stepping across the sand and onto the soft grass, a cool summer breeze floated between the palm trees and over the pools of flowing sky blue water. As her feet touched the sumptuous ground, she heard unseen voices softly murmuring and beautiful songs welcoming her. She let her hand drop slowly to touch the flowing water, but pulled back, hesitating, unsure. Contemplating the possibility of this reality, the questions emerged. *Could this be real? Will I be disappointed again? Will this beauty disappear before me, or is this truly my* oasis? Allowing her frail fingertips to fall, the moment she touched the water she knew the truth. The boundless love that flowed forth from her heart was real!

In the midst of the harsh, unyielding desert, she surrendered completely, and with a sweet smile of contentment she immersed herself in the beautiful blue waters of the oasis. Instantly, a tremendous transformation began. It felt as if her old body was being washed away, and as she arose from the depths of the water, a wondrous miracle occurred. The maiden's youth, vitality, and beauty had been restored, and, with this, she became One with her soul. Her spirit *knew* that even though her life appeared to be one of endless wandering, it was not endless at all. She had ascended through the wisdom of the journey to become one with the all-encompassing love that had always been within her. Her transformation was complete and she reveled in pure ecstasy, having become the radiant personification of beauty itself!

Turning to show the Bedouin the miraculous events that had happened, all she saw was the camel, only the camel standing there, waiting. To her amazement, she was gleaming with an Ethereal Light that radiated in all directions. Somehow, she knew this was the Light of the Bedouin, and in that glorious instant of transcendence the two had become One. At last, it was clear that all along it had been her Higher Self, in the form of the Bedouin, who had pointed the way home to her heart's desire. *Her entire life had been transformed from the meaningless to the authentic vision of her true self.*

The camel had also been transformed, and where it once stood there appeared a gleaming white stallion. The waters of the oasis had overflowed, reaching out beyond the horizon and beautifying the entire desert before her with its vitality and lushness. A new land, reaching as far as the eye could see, had been created, a land that reflected radiant love.

In an instant, she found herself atop the majestic stallion, which had become symbolic of her elevation into this beautiful new experience. Pausing to drink in this moment of transformation, she felt radiant, blissful, and beatific. It was then, and only then, that she could embrace the knowledge that she was fully awake and truly alive.

There, through the maiden's retelling of this tale in that timeless moment of contemplation, I felt a deep kinship as I had envisioned how her personal transformation occurred. Certainly, in my own life, I had faced many similar experiences while chasing the illusions of Maya. I knew the feeling only too well of having pursued a hope or dream, only to find that, like snow on a summer's day, it melted away before my eyes. So many times, I had also been disappointed, almost always by my own foolishness. These were the times in my own life that led me toward believing the dream or vision was real. But too often the dream was only a fantasy, an illusion of my own making. I identified closely with the maiden's trials and struggles to find the truth. As her story unfolded, I thought of the many times I had searched for my own oasis. In similar fashion, the longings of how I wanted my life to be disappeared right before me. I had come to know the truth is not an elusive dream. Always there and ever-present, divine truth can only be found and mastered through experiencing the deepest love within. This journey can only be grasped through expanded wisdom and awareness from within our hearts.

The emotional depth of that inner vision embracing this new truth expanded through the center of my heart. Her story, which had become a rendering of my own life, was one of the most beautiful I had ever heard and can only be described as utterly sublime.

The appearance and true intention of this beautiful

woman of light and the message she brought began to resonate within me:

"Before you lies one of life's greatest adventures. This is a time you will treasure always, for at last your destiny is revealed. Even grander will be the magnificence of its realization. You will travel further than you ever have, to look upon the face of the Grand Being from which all Creation emanates. Awaiting you is an experience so magnificent and so profound that no words can speak of its splendor. Coming to once again proclaim the call, Love will always lead, showing the way."

The feelings and emotions of this spectacular moment flowed into me and ecstasy vibrated every part of my heart. Every revelation of her extraordinary message resonated within me, and I realized that I was also glowing with the essence of her light.

Smiling, my eyes were drawn toward the bright luminous clouds appearing before me, and somehow I knew this would be my new path.

THE MAN IN THE COPPER DISH

Focusing intently on the bright clouds becoming even more visible, I felt as if I was drawn out of my physical body and into them. As the clouds parted, I could see a beautiful shimmering island in the midst of a sparkling blue ocean.

It felt like I was floating down to the beach. There, I saw a narrow flight of old stairs attached to a wooden railing leading up to the top of a small mound. I felt compelled to move on, and made my way up a few steps until I reached the top. Gazing out, I was startled to see what appeared to be a huge copper dish spanning a tremendous distance. Actually, it looked more like a theatre in the round. Looking into the center of the dish, I saw a man of the same shade of copper seated in the middle, and I made my way to where he was.

I sat next to him and he began showing me something. He breathed in and out, taking very slow and deliberate breaths. As he inhaled, his image became lighter, and translucent. In releasing his breath, his full image reappeared. I found that I could do the same, but not to the same degree, at first. Then, all of a sudden, we were breathing together as One and we began to materialize at the edge of the dish.

It was an incredible sensation. Although still in the middle of the dish, we were also at the edge, simultaneously! I sat there trying to grasp what was happening, and then it happened again. Continuing to be seated in the middle, a third appearance of us occurred on the other side of the dish.

I looked wildly at the man in copper, hoping he would offer some explanation, but he did not. This continued to happen, over and over again, until the entire outer rim of the dish was lined with our images, exactly as we were in the middle. Our individualities, from the center to the edges, were manifesting in perfect synchronicity. I was surprised to realize the images were not copies or reflections of me—*they were me!* I could be any one of them, or all of them simultaneously. I was everywhere and connected to everything, all in the same instant, the same breath. In witnessing this extraordinary sight, I realized that all of life occurs in the same eternal moment and exists in all alternate dimensions, at the same time. What an awe-inspiring revelation!

Finally the man spoke to me, simply asking a single question. "Of all the images that you see, do you know which one is the **real** you?"

I hesitated for a moment and then gasped, "All of them."

He merely nodded but appeared to be pleased.

After maintaining this state a while longer and then gently returning to our singular images, we were once again in the middle of the dish. This was the most liberating of my experiences, up to now. The man in copper remained seated and smiling. He instructed me further and suggested I explore the beauty of the inner island.

Moving deeper into this haven, I had the feeling of passing through a veil, although none was visible. I soon discovered the island to be a veritable paradise, with many different types of Beings coming and going. I believed I was meeting them for the very first time, yet somehow they seemed to know me quite well. It was very lively and joyful, as I found myself interacting with Beings I had never seen, even though we had always occupied the same space.

Converging at an incredible port of arrival, there were many who had journeyed from destinations far and wide. Their arrivals were announced in vibrational tapestries of color and light, which were the very *emanations* of each visitor. Filled with ever-changing mosaics of sound, the space around us was woven and blended in perfect harmony with each arrival.

It was beautiful and magical.

MEETING MY MESSENGERS

The Sage

The joyful feelings of having met such incredible Beings still swirled around me, as I strolled down one of the paths leading deeper into the island. I came upon a lovely dwelling nestled in a wooded grove. Approaching, I saw a small cottage that seemed rather modest from the outside. The door opened, inviting me to enter. A brilliant light shone, increasing into many rooms as I stepped through the door. Standing there in amazement, the dimensions continued to expand, becoming immense. A huge statue seated in one of the enormous rooms immediately sprang to life to greet me. At first, I was taken aback, but then I was pleasantly surprised because he was beaming a warm welcoming smile. He can only be described as a Being whose face radiated a natural sense of enlightenment, etched with the wisdom of many ages.

Because of an unmistakable air of truth about him, I followed him down a wide hallway that was brightly lit with fragrant candles. I was unafraid as he guided me into an even larger adjoining chamber that was reminiscent of a sprawling cathedral. Lifting the golden scepter in his hand, he *illuminated* the walls surrounding us, and I could see many murals depicting past civilizations. Motioning me to look closer, I was startled as each scene began to move and come to life. Fascinated by the spectacle of seeing these events unfolding in time, it took me a moment to comprehend what he was showing me. In every living portrait, I saw humanity again and again, in civilization after civilization, epoch after epoch.

Moving very rapidly, whole periods of history passed before our eyes in minutes. Suddenly the Sage would freeze the moment and the room was instantly transformed into the actual time and place. Although the lives were varied and many, they were related and interrelated.

I was watching a remarkable unfoldment. There were moments of my own life when visions and memories of such experiences had come to me. I had relived fragments of other lives and other times long since passed. They were as real as any memory could be, but they were fleeting and had no context within which to place them. Now I understood how my soul was linked to the unfolding currents of life, appearing in age after age, and although each life was unique, the underlying *intention* always remained the same. Through countless struggles and triumphs beyond the limitations of time, I saw my animated soul continually bringing to bear the universal truths that are part of the fabric of all civilizations.

As each life came and went, it was astonishing to observe how humanity arose and fell in cycles of evolution, yet so often the end result would be drastically different. In some instances, I saw civilizations that forever clashed in wars, darkness, and destruction, ultimately descending into their own devastation. Yet, there were others who had been reborn anew. These had become known through many myths and fables as the *Golden Ages*, a time when peace and abundance flourished for all life. From the densest energy imaginable, transforming into the most refined and beautiful attainment of spirit's evolution, I witnessed the great cycles of our planetary history and the journey of all life. It was all visible right before my eyes.

Inevitably, as a result of some great natural catastrophe or self-inflicted destruction, even the highest most aware cultures came to their end. I found it puzzling that as most of the civilizations crumbled, there was a mysterious loss of memory and knowledge. Clawing their way upward from the remnants of the past, complete new beginnings had to be forged. Each arc of life would awaken and grow out of the darkness, and then ultimately create or discover unique ways to once again reach the Light. New waves of civilizations would rise and fall as millennia came and went. Every age embraced the continuing unfolding of its unique destiny. What majesty!

As I watched these grand cycles unfolding, I began to notice a very subtle and delicate image arcing from beginning to end, across the horizon of each epoch. Each age evolved slowly, and as millennia passed my vision continued to grow until I could clearly see the captivating appearance of an exquisite Divine Being, shining in dazzling elegance. Faintly distinguishable at first, a ray of light, unique in color, shone forth from within its own aura, increasing in power and glory as the epoch was reaching its peak. As it flowed through from a different dimension, no individual on the planet's surface was consciously aware of this radiance. Yet, I could see it and I knew the eternal Presence was there, continually nourishing our world with blessings and light.

These Master Beings evolved with each age, resembling those who had once inhabited our planet from ancient civilizations in a distant forever, long ago. Some of them reflected a masculine identity; others expressed the universal feminine; still others were a perfectly blended embodiment of both. On rare occasions, there was more than one at a time and it seemed obvious they were all deeply connected in a grand spiritual calling.

These indescribable Beings possessed features that appeared heavenly, even celestial, but nevertheless they also possessed human qualities, expressing the greatest attributes of both. It was definitely apparent that they had once walked the planet themselves. As masters who had long since been elevated beyond the limitations of their own evolution, they continued to resonate with the planetary souls who were still on the path to enlightenment.

Over and again the spiral of life would turn. When each age reached its divine fruition, humanity and Masters would complete their journey as a new epoch was born and a new dance of life would begin. These transcendent ones, having fulfilled their own evolutionary mission, were gloriously transformed, ascending to realms beyond. Yet, out of profound compassion, these multidimensional Beings chose to remain throughout time as the loving guardians of each age of humanity.

Visible to us only because of this suspended moment, literally hundreds of thousands of years in the world of time and space passed before our eyes. Occasionally some of the more enlightened of humanity did begin to feel or intuit the unseen presence of the Ascended Ones. In these instances, their lives were greatly enhanced by the sheer love they attracted.

Throughout the ages there have been many who have lost their way and looked to these Master Teachers as saints, holy ones, or prophets, beseeching them for guidance and help in lighting the way. In the most difficult of times, hoping to be given the answer or delivered from the darkness, they have cried out, "Will the light come today, or perhaps tomorrow?" Will our deliverance soon arrive? Each Ascended Master, from every age, heard the cries and pleas and was deeply moved in compassion and empathy, always seeking to soothe each troubled soul through the expression of love. Yet, they knew that all of us must awaken to see and become the true breath of life on our own. For surely if these masters held only passing reflections, or perhaps even the greatest wisdom of all life, these mysteries could not be revealed until their time of truth had come. Having been through similar journeys themselves, even they would not have it so.

THE PRIESTESS

The wise Sage vanished and I found myself in a towering dome-shaped temple where a new guide awaited me. She appeared as a mysterious and all-knowing Priestess, with beams of rippling colors emanating from her. Approaching me, she shifted into an elevated state of awareness and expressed an intense effervescent field of vibrant energy that surrounded us completely. Laying her hand on my shoulder and raising her crystal wand upward into this field, she attracted a powerful magnetic vibration, revealing entirely new emerging ages that had not yet come to be.

Shining forth before us, generations of new realities were evolving forward into the future on brilliant waves of light. It was as if an ocean was flowing into and out of me. With each successive crest of collective evolution, I could see even more development and more blessings of greater awareness, awakening the deepest levels of universal consciousness. She touched my forehead with her fingertips, and in a brilliant flash I could see closer and deeper, bringing into clarity the finest of details.

It was awe-inspiring to see what I somehow knew was only one of the many beautiful directions humanity could actualize. As the future extended out in front of me, I saw that each new age had its own Master Being, elegantly evolving over each passing epoch. Slowly materializing above each forthcoming generation, they created new expansive advancements to bring about love and peace for the benefit of all. Ever so gently as in the past, emerging as guardians of each monumental era, they poured forth in an endless sea of possibility, moving infinitely across the ocean of conscious evolution. As our vision flowed on to new horizons, each Being ascending into mastery became even more magnificent than the one preceding it.

Through faith and devotion, clearly their watchfulness was also evolving and ever-expanding, patiently waiting until each age reached its pinnacle. At precisely the exact instant each epoch flowered into its zenith, they would mysteriously emerge and delicately assist or aid in the transition from each age into the next. In that divine moment, they became the perfect puzzle piece, the last splash of perfected colors, completing the glorious portrait of life's direction. For so long, the masters had awaited our expansion into the Light. Now, marking the fulfillment of their heartfelt mission, they became one with us. They were the beacons lighting the path. Through their total giving, we had come to know our own fulfillment and discovered our own way. These eternal ones, each more beautiful than the last, were like exquisite flowers mysteriously blooming in the darkness of a winter's moon, yet somehow blossoming in all their glory to greet the dawn of each new spring.

Motioning for me to look even closer, I was entranced as my guide once again brought the vision of each evolutionary scheme to its full brilliance. I felt as though I was standing on a mountaintop viewing the entirety of evolution flowing by in all directions in an infinite ever-flowing river of life.

All the Ascended Masters who had ever been present throughout the entire history of this world appeared simultaneously. It was an astonishing sight as the total range of my ability to experience seemed to extend into creation itself. My guide paused in reverence at this vision of majesty and love. Raising her arm skyward, the heavens opened to reveal new dimensions in layer upon layer as far as the eye could see. At this point, I came to realize a great and far-reaching truth.

These Master Beings in wave after wave seemed to stretch out to infinity, and I knew it could only mean one thing. Since the evolution of these Ascended Masters was inextricably woven with our own, there must also be multilayered waves of evolving humanity that stretch out to infinity, as well.

I was speechless as I witnessed the loving support of these champions of humanity, who had walked the planet themselves eons ago. Out of pure devotion they had chosen to remain, even after achieving their own mastery. My heart opened to the full scope of love that flows out and blesses us, as time-enhanced, ascending mortals, and I heard myself exclaim: *We are so loved!*

Witnessing this endless parallel evolution of

humanity and Masters, these ascended bodhisattvas offered living proof of the heights we can reach. As their images became even more glorious and radiant, rippling away from us, they also became less and less familiar as they extended to the unseen horizon.

THE JEWEL

Now, the crowning jewel of my visit was dawning. The wise Sage reappeared and, with The Priestess, we three joined as one. Viewing the vastness of life's panorama, encompassing the fullness of my soul's journeys and the enlightened promised of a future yet to come, an electrifying experience occurred. There, with only the three of us as witnesses to the eternal presence of that timeless moment, all life... past, present, and future became one glorious vision. As I looked up and out to view the ever-unfolding worlds of time and space present at every stage of every age, I perceived the boundless, breathtaking Spiral of Life's Creation. Perpetually ascending ever so slightly, with rare instances of sudden turns upward, it revealed that no matter the circumstances affecting each passing epoch, there is always an ongoing progression of enlightenment and awakening. We stood in the center of the ever-expanding worlds of space-time as the wondrous Spiral of Life Creation slowly spun over and around us, and into the infinite regions beyond.

In that moment, with no visible beginning or end to embrace, my heart could truly see that all life is an eternal, ever-evolving outpouring of ecstatic love, ever becoming creation upon greater creation. This ultimate vision of truth was stunning to behold!

As my messengers elevated my awareness even higher, the masters and the vision of the great Spiral of Life's Evolution were revealed as towering symbols of eternity. Spanning the countless civilizations of my spirit's journey, I beheld the transcendent timelessness of my own higher essence. It became apparent that the seemingly mysterious conditions of my own life had been but preparation for something greater. Now what I had learned from my past experiences could be implemented to create and express all I saw before me.

Through this gift of witnessing events of the passing eons and the deep insight these experiences granted, I was given a glimpse into what was about to follow.

I saw myself in the midst of masses of humanity, connected through a heart circuit of intertwining love. Brilliant rays of coloration were washing through, bathing and touching all who were gathered. *My heart was immersed in the outpouring light of love's realization.* Some from within the massive gatherings were touched deeply and moved to rapture, as their hearts united within this outpouring and joy of love's light.

Others arising from our midst appeared to have been reborn as they took their place, uniting with the masses who had also sought the highest of truth. They became beacons of the new way, shining and elevating the spirits of those whose experiences had brought them to the place where but the sheerest veil remained.

In the distance, I could see many others who were, like myself, radiating love freely. Uplifting those who were able to hold this sacred truth in their hearts, they shone fiercely to dispel the darkness from those who were still in doubt. We flowed onward like a mighty river, until all had become beacons of truth and light!

THE CHOICE

Once again our focus shifted back into the immense hall, as this journey with my guides and enlightened ones was moving to completion. the Sage bid farewell, having dramatically rolled back the barriers of time and history to reveal all of humanity's past struggles and advancements. The Priestess smiled, and I felt our hearts connect in a vision of the beauty that lay ahead. Having shown the promise of future possibilities, she also ascended back into a horizon of ever-changing light and energy.

I felt a great passion begin to surge within. Wave after wave of spiraling emotion radiated from within me. I could see the shapes of the vibrations as they rippled away, flowing beyond my sight. Vibrating within ever-expanding circles of color and light, they inspired me to reach higher, giving birth to even greater vision. These experiences continued expanding on and on, seemingly to infinity.

I was immersed in incredibly beautiful images that reflected ever-changing color, mood, feeling, and emotion, all soaring and intermingling within one another. In this moment, I was surrounded by everything I could possibly know and be.

Remembering what my guides from the halls of past and future had revealed, I knew the ultimate quest would be the one that awakens our true nature and brings us all into unity. Knowing that we are messengers of abundance and possess the same wealth, from deep within came the call to go forth and help in whatever way possible to reveal the wonders that lie within each of us.

The oneness of humanity burst upon me in an exalted flash of transformational revelation. In that divine instant, I felt love streaming forth from my heart, connecting me to every soul throughout all creation. I witnessed the multitudes who embraced the desire to discover their totality and become the realization of their highest truth. Even those who were unaware of any of it, uncaring and indifferent, toiling away in a state of waking sleep, were included. Every last man, woman, and child mattered, because to deny any, to leave even one out, would be to deny a part of myself and the whole of the Grand Creation.

The splendor was glorious as we united in an exalted moment. All of our individual souls blended into a state of oneness; yet they retained and celebrated their diversity and uniqueness. Collective individuality merged in oneness. This was the awareness of personal being, within and through the Being of One.

Seeing what was possible, the choice was mine alone to make. I could continue my quest in a personal fashion as an individual, or I could go forth to become a messenger of light, seeking to help uplift those, who like myself, sought the experience of life's most profound mysteries.

By revealing that all of humanity is united as One, the wise Sage and the mysterious Priestess had given me the greatest of gifts. I also knew it would not be until the truth of love shines through all of humanity that we will become the masters of life, divinely designed by the intention of our creation.

As the deep remembrance of our starry birthright stirs within us, we once again come to know the truth. Separation is, and has always been, an illusion.

DESTINY'S REALIZATION

Finding myself once again in the copper dish, I knew I had been shown all that was possible for me to know, for the moment. Bidding farewell to the man in copper and this paradise of revelation, the song of my heart called me onward.

Strains of beautiful music echoed as I made my way. Images of glorious moments flashed around me. Waves of the purest bliss rippled through me, and I softly murmured, "I will not turn away from anyone who wishes to have such an experience." I became devoted to do whatever possible, vowing from the height and breadth of my soul to assist in the flight of freedom to any and all who wished it! Forever striving to achieve this goal, and perpetually expressing love's soaring light, I would surrender to the truth shining brilliantly through me. Becoming a beacon, a torch of truth assisting all life in receiving love's radiant light, was now the call of my spirit.

For love, once realized, will ultimately inspire each of us to unite as one people. Becoming the family of Humanity, we will not rest until we know, from whence we come and where we go, and what must be done to make it so.

Striving then, to bring light into darkness, wisdom into confusion, love into living, and unity into life...
We go forth....

TRANSCENDENT CONSCIOUSNESS

Chapter Two

BEING ALL

PRELUDE

In giving rise to our ability to see that "past and future" are one, the attainment of transformational consciousness has become our rite of passage. Journeying on now together it is the sense of the collective We, filling each of us with excitement and a new sense of wonder. Elevating our sights beyond these life-altering revelations, our perceptions begin to embrace new possibilities of even higher dimensions as the promise of greater beauty now beckons.

Dazzling scenes sparkling faintly in the distance are leading us ever onward. Although our sensitivity has become even more expansive, these far-off visions still seem impossible at first. Suddenly a shimmering light bridge appears, extending outward and upward, drawing us to new horizons and the thrill of distant discoveries. Our awareness is being enticed into the higher frequencies of transcendence. We feel an awakening akin to emerging from a dense forest into a sunny meadow. Thoughts, words and language pale, giving birth to new inspirations seeking to grasp the essence of this new land now calling serenely to us.

THE JOURNEY

From this bright light of ascendancy, reaching for the highest within ourselves, illuminating our way ahead, we spiral open like flowers rising to the sun.

We are becoming buoyant and brighter, as slowly the intensity of our emanations begins to expand. Feeling the slightest touch of a breeze at our back, we serenely expand through an ephemeral bath of sumptuous colors. Our sights are set on loftier realms, as we rise up into a bright shining sky of azure blue that commands our entire view.

Suddenly breaking through the billowy clouds, we see the magnificent breathtaking summits of a snow-capped mountain range, ablaze in glistening crests reflecting a golden shimmer, surrounded by a low lying mist of iridescent rose.

Just then, we pass over the first peaks. There! Do you see it? As we move closer, suspended between the spectacular peaks, we see an exquisite City of Sparkling Light.

TRASARA

Before us, rising out of a flourishing green valley deep within the surrounding mountains, is the skyline of a brilliant shining city with spires sculpted of light. The architecture and structures are veritable works of living art, each perfect unto itself. There are towers, steeples, and other flowing dwellings that have no definitive contour, yet they maintain a fluidity of motion that continually fashions them into countless ever-changing creations.

Everything looks to be an idea that has been energized into being. Nothing is opaque. The city exudes a genuine quality of elasticity and aliveness. These captivating contours are at once translucent, but they seem to have substance. We can see through the unique textures of energized color, even as they retain their individual purity.

Floating under the bluest of skies, radiance surrounds the entire city and there is sweet music in the air. Every creation is highly luminous and emits its own unique tone and glow, producing a feeling of lushness, blending perfectly with all.

Let us stroll down a street. Look there! That flashing light! It went by so fast. And look! There's another and another, and yet another! Like shooting stars in all directions they fly!

OUR GUIDE

Suddenly one of the streaming lights stops next to us, and in an instant it transforms into the image of a man. His features are outlined in light, yet they are clearly visible and seem to be perfect in every detail. He smiles gently at us.

Without using words, he somehow conveys a greeting, "Welcome to Trasara."

"One of the qualities Trasarans share is the ability to project whatever likeness we wish. Our individual identities exist solely in the spirit of our own essence. Having command over all forms of expression, we merely envision our desired appearance. Allow me to show you the wonders of our city."

We move into a plaza of incredible beauty. Ethereal music dances around us, displaying exalted color arrays, intermingling with luxuriant fragrances. We can see and feel these scents, sights, and sounds.

Uniquely created, elegant towers seem to rise from everywhere, surrounding us with glistening vibrant colors. The interactions are taking place within, as well as among these creations in ever-changing mosaics displaying a ceaseless interplay of light and sound. These structures are somehow animated by the same flow of energy, and as we view their interactions, we feel the strange sensation of spilling past our boundaries, creating an almost "out-of-body" experience.

Our guide seems to feel our bewilderment and reassures us, "All is well. Life on Trasara is spent experiencing inspired soul expressions through the universal act of creation. The mighty Being with whom we are one, is constantly energizing our needs. No one has more than another, for each possesses the unconditional potential to become whatever they desire. Living totally in essence and having evolved past the idea of lack, we are no longer occupied with worry and concern."

We can only stare at him in wide-eyed amazement!
Our guide continues...

"All Trasarans give completely, shining forth through their own individuality as each seeks to uplift the quality of our individual and collective life. The challenge of our journey is creating anything and everything that brings us closer to the highest shining light of Love.

"You are viewing innumerable participants working in accord for the betterment of all. Some have chosen to help in designing the environment, while others dedicate their lives to the ongoing renewal and originality of our lifestyle. Many share a faithful devotion to the transformation of new ideas into the reality of our collective advancement. Teachers of every conceivable endeavor are helping to uplift those who are striving to rise up and meet their individual potential. In this continuing unfolding, we are genuinely exuberant as we go about the tasks of designing and co-creating life and living as One.

"As you continue your visit through our city you are likely to find the multiplicity of the many wonders we have conceived, very exciting. We have developed our abilities in varying degrees, yet the most brilliant among us are continuously and selflessly reaching out to Trasara, that all can receive help and guidance. There are many different lifestyles and achievements along our path, nonetheless we are all Trasarans by birthright and each individual is valued and honored equally."

Everywhere we look happiness is reflected in the radiant glow of these unique and brilliant Beings. Our guide seems delighted by our joy-filled observations of this wondrous land.

He points ahead and we *feel* him tells us, "Come... let us continue. There is so much to see."

Suddenly many loving Trasarans encircle us, lifting us to a slightly more expansive vista point that reveals the exquisite beauty of the entire city lying before us. Gazing in fascination, we realize this paradise is a glorious tribute to the extraordinary creative inspiration and universal unity by which this entire race has reached unimaginable heights.

Now, suspended above the rose mist surrounding the city, yet another awe-inspiring sight materializes!

THE GLOBES

We see immense spheres of light all around us. They are the gleaming Globes of Trasara. Each is made of what looks to be living fire that emanates light, but not heat.

Every globe is rare in color and resplendence, each resonating its own individual harmony in perfect unison with the others. The globes are sending out rays of brilliantly colored light in every direction, permeating everything they touch. This blush of luminosity shines throughout all. At times, the globes look to be superimposed over one another through energy unknown to us. Somehow, they retain their individual purity, while moving perfectly in a limitless flow through all the others.

Similar in size to a full moon on our world, the globes continually amplify their resonance. Orbiting much closer to the surface of the city, they look to be tethered as they cycle in their trajectory. Each has an individual glow, an ethereal quality that illuminates their shimmering outline.

We see flashes of light beams, similar to our guide's first arrival, flying toward, then absorbed into the globes. This further enhances their brilliance and adds to their splendor.

Our guide enlightens us....

"The globes are in constant motion, as each beams out its own unique message of grace to all Trasara. They do not, however, possess an intrinsic form. All globes become the vibrational shape the gatherings resonate into expression. In this instance, they only resemble globes, the simplest of universal forms, as they reflect the billions of Trasarans who have gathered. Each Trasaran who enters into union with a particular globe lends their spirit to that singular desire, purpose, and intention.

"Every globe rotates in perfect synchronicity with Trasara, imbuing our entire landscape with the qualities of their individual light rays. Trasarans absorb these qualities directly and their spirits are perpetually nourished and uplifted.

"The globes are made up of countless individual Trasarans who work together in unity. By projecting the love in their hearts and the aspirations of their lives in concert, they greatly increase the magnitude of their combined desires. In this ecstatic manner they are able to tap into and become one with the single source of truth that guides all creations of consciousness.

"Look at the exquisite Rose Globe as it expands clearly into view. Feel the ripples of emotion exuding from its deepest wells. Ecstasy of exhilarating passion pours from those whose hearts are bursting with compassion for their race. The most delicate shades of rose glow from within and permeate the atmosphere itself. The colors of the globe ripple out on emotional waves of pink, lavender, fuchsia, and deeply rich red. They are constantly in touch with all life. By reflecting these qualities unconditionally, they shine throughout. The Beings of the Rose Globe are engaged in the act of originating only the purest expression of love. By infusing their individualities in unity, the ecstasy is expanded to all of Trasara.

"Feel the frequency shift now into the luminous Golden Globe, the effusion of wisdom and knowledge. As it shines, its message, as with all the globes, is reflected universally. Absorbed to the deepest extent possible, the luster of the Golden Globe reaches all Trasarans seeking to experience the exaltation of Universal Mind. Through this unity, the grandest Trasaran ideals are embellished without constraints. Here they strive to surpass their individual limitations, and in communion with those of one mind, attain their finest awareness."

"Orbiting next into view, is the mighty Violet Globe. Trasarans who have evolved into supreme levels of divine communication find themselves to be in direct harmony with the highest vibrational emanation of Source. In a compassionate desire to attain that soaring state of grace, they strive to become free and effortless vehicles of higher will. Benevolence, sympathy, and kindness are their aspirations, and these qualities are enhanced and expanded to their highest measure, showing the most far-reaching insight into our collective consciousness. Of all the globes, the Violet Globe most closely identifies the direction of our destiny.

"Each globe is original in scope and inner working, yet along with its attuned participants, their unique intention is constantly evolving. Individuals are freely merging as one, transmuting their life essence into effortless balance through the magnitude of their collective highest vision.

"There are also myriads of other unique luminosities and shapes passing by that are combinations of all you see. These are evolving tones and shades just emerging, as Trasarans move on to new inspirations. They can spend as much or as little time in the globes of their choice, or openly choose to pursue their own unique dreams. Whatever they choose, all remain in touch and forever connected. Ever-expanding the whole of Trasara, the outpouring of these spheres perpetually streams forth the highest qualities of authentic truth."

How beautiful it all seems....

"I invite you to look even closer now. With pure intention, you can see a faint outline of the Globe of White. It is unattainable by most, and accessible to only a handful of Trasarans. We feel the White Globe is a gateway through which we may pass onward to the next state of being. You will learn more of the nature of the White Globe as our journey progresses.

"Through cooperation and innovative aspiration, every choice is divine. No matter what endeavor an individual aspires to, it is always with the intention of becoming the most glorious expression of love. This is our way, forging ahead to experience ever-expanding cycles of possibility and attunement with Source."

Smiling, our guide senses our fascination with the globes and Trasara. He continues….

"The globes are a reflection of the unified quality of character we share. Our way is to amplify our collective desires and aspirations in the greatest fashion. Once attained, there continues to be the singular path that many travel in hope of creating an even finer quality of life beyond what are merely these transient stops."

Pausing for a moment, our focus shifts. We turn to our guide, who can see the question in our eyes, and we ask, "What we are witnessing here is truly amazing, but there seems to be something missing and we cannot help but wonder. In our world the elements of desire, love, and passion are dominant forces, affecting and touching almost every aspect of our unfolding lives. Do they also reside here in your exalted midst?"

THE LOVERS

Two Beings materialize before us. They are enfolded completely within a brilliant cloak of lucent light. We feel their heart waves drawing them closer to each other. The light surrounding them begins to pulsate as waves of emotion stream forth. *Disappearing within a swirl of love, they emerge as one image, which is a perfect blending of both.* The totality of each essence has merged into wholeness, infusing this oneness with their highest love.

Intimately experiencing and becoming one with the very heart of the other, they look to be the ultimate reflection of true lovers. Their emotions are intertwining, playing out in a dance of passion and caress made visible by the sheer glory of the united oneness of their hearts' desire.

All is known and felt by each in divine union, as they give everything, surrendering into bliss, reveling in the fullness of knowing the other. Loving becomes an act of deepest communion in which they shine forth unabashedly, seeking their united beauty of deepest personal love. Radiance simply beams forth in excitement, intimacy, and desire from these two, who have become one. As the unity of these lovers reaches its highest pinnacle, the swirls from which we first viewed their emergence wash over us for a precious moment. Through them, we are given the gift of feeling the bliss of ecstasy. Having merged in rapturous oneness, scintillating ever so delicately, they ascend, spiraling out of our view into their own evanescence of enchantment and ecstasy.

Through the revelation of our newly heightened vision of love, another shining dimension of exhilaration has been awakened within us and made to shine. Love and passion are alive and thriving on Trasara!

THE MORES

Our guide beams as he reveals the most awe-inspiring truth of this land. "Transcendence through creativity is the heart and soul of Trasara. This is the mighty pillar our way of life is built upon. Travelers along the Great Way who have been guided here are able to see this very truth is to be one of many possible ways forward. The act of creation is indeed a reflection of the greatest of all creators, Source.

"We will fly on now to gaze upon those who have achieved the most exceptional heights. Overcoming their once personal limitations, they are the most extraordinary among us. Attaining outright mastery of their gifts, soaring far beyond even our most expansive imagination, they have triumphantly journeyed to the farthest reaching spirals of a transcendent new dawn."

Our guide raises his eyes, and instantly many gleaming Trasarans encircle us and transport us to the highest peaks overlooking the dazzling city below.

ETHEREAL ARTISTS

Upon our arrival we are amazed to see the great distance we have traveled...in just an instant. It takes us a moment to focus as our view from here is truly astonishing. What a thrilling sight!

We drink in the brilliant images of ethereal artists creating huge portraits of living light, floating above the many glistening crests surrounding us. We watch, mesmerized as these artists mix soul energies into unique colors and combinations reflecting the desire of their ingenious hearts. Glowing brushes gracefully sweep across floating palettes, as otherworldly hues bring forth grand works of art that are the embodiment of their most heartfelt authentic inner vision. Commanding the most profound acts of creativity and aligned with fantastical forms of malleable energy, their achievements are forever reaching outward to the infinite. Their singular vision is dedicated to the genesis of their individual universal masterpiece. Ever-expanding in beauty and emotional power, they unceasingly reach toward their own transcendence.

Our perceptions have been filled to the brim of our capacity. We cannot hope to understand the enthralling spectacle overwhelming our senses, yet we cannot turn away from this hypnotic dance of creation.

Mixed and multi-media art, abstract architectural illuminations, and sculptures unfold before us, as well as ongoing experimental imaginings of avant-garde Spirit creations. Every magnificent piece carries its own exclusive vibrational identity, as energy pours through each artist's divine will to become a one-of-a-kind *work of heart.* It is deeply moving to see the living nature of these creative outpourings, combining love and light, energy and desire, blending all into the beauty of sound, idea, color, and even captivating fragrance.

Though we observe varying degrees of ability, there is not the slightest hint of competition. Each master is both a student of life and a teacher to those of beginning or advanced expertise. All gifts are divinely bestowed and equally honored. There have been countless representations of talent along our way, but it is not until we reach this grand master level that we can see what is, to us, the miraculous. The greatest dream of all is to rise up to the achievements of the Grand Masters, who bring to life and manifest transcendence through creativity in ways no other has yet to conceive.

The mysterious unnoticed truth is these elevated artists have discovered unknown ways to splash their ethereal canvases with the full spectrum of all colors and frequencies. By embracing these techniques even before they begin, they are nearly limitless in their scope of vibrational alchemy.

Our guide continues… "The images that arise are awakened from the profound vision emerging from these virtuosos. They are born through the very depths of their souls. The light-colors create the palettes from the deepest pools of their visionary spirit. As the artists synchronize in perfected focus with their inner vision, images begin to magically appear on their canvases. They are the exact mirrored reflection of the artist's conceptions, sensitivity, imagination, and love. These grand revelations of soul, surpassing all former concepts of perfection, are the result of eternal inspiration. They bring forth the living works that become their monumental life masterpieces."

Spread out before us, this vista of beauty takes our breath away. As our vision begins to adjust to these wonders, and we start to comprehend what appear to be unfolding miracles, our senses are elevated once again. Just as we witness the final brushstroke, the last chisel and polish of one full complete work of art, another new divine masterpiece springs to life. In the most enthralling of experiences, we see the continuing grand procession of the treasures of Trasara, but now they have transcended their original conception. In perfect unison with the advent of their final completeness, *we hear the paintings sing as they rise up off their canvases and spring to life.*

The artistry on Trasara has been reborn, displaying in dance and euphoric harmonies the intricacies of their created images as song poems, becoming the very rapture of imagery itself. This wondrous unfolding of artistic mastery leaves us full of excitement and wonder.

Obviously tuned into this very moment, our guide dramatically affirms, "Yes. The colors, figures, carvings, and sculpted creations are set into motion, ultimately reaching the stage of development at which they begin a vibrational dance, swaying in unknown rhythms through the frequencies of the artist's soul inspiration. Pictures, murals, and portraits, previously seen as paintings on a canvas and once inanimate sculptures, have come alive in spontaneous bursts of life.

"These fervently inspired creations of the heart defy our concepts of possibility because of the artist's use of *soul-centered will,* as they command unseen energies to be expressed into form. All of the creations originate from the artist's visions. The conceptual inspiration of each one compels the primal forces of their inherent gifts of creativity to rise above former limitations bringing forth their crowning tour de force.

"The most mystical of events, however, occurs at the time of the triumphant glorious consummation such as this. Once the master's work has reached its pinnacle of near perfection, there is a celestial outpouring of illumination and instantly the artist disappears into the Globe of White Light. Though gone from our sight, the artist's presence remains connected to us and continues to communicate through their work. But now they exist in a state of transcendence we cannot yet perceive. Through having attained this very degree of ascendancy, the Grand Master is granted passage through the gateless gate into brilliant and eternal dimensions.

"At the very moment the celebrated Grand Master vanishes, their first protégé comes forth in beautiful synergy and steps into the master role, becoming the next most accomplished and revered. This cycle of becoming continues without pause, and all know they will attain their own divine perfection. At that moment they will also ascend the path to forever." We contemplate this marvelous Trasaran cycle of becoming, transfixed in reverence.

Delicately descending ever so slightly our companions move us below the Trasaran skyline. There we become aware the City of Light has expanded before us and taken on continental proportions. Still marveling at how there can be such excellence of design, in the distance we hear music singing its way toward us on enchanted winds. We are called to follow the sensuous sounds echoing from the valleys below.

As we draw closer, we see composers conducting glorious unseen orchestras in stunning symphonies. Our hearts feel the vibratory power of the music resounding over wide chasms of natural amphitheaters that stretch across unfathomable domains. We feel the pure resonance of these refrains reaching out to further distances than any we've ever known or could otherwise have envisioned. Employing these naturally perfect formations in this ingenious way profoundly enhances the acoustics and produces a quality of tonal originality unlike any other. The reverberation of each glorious masterpiece completely fills the space surrounding it, permeating all with its magnificent purity of expression, as it rises up from the valley of its origin. Our guide's eyes close, "You must listen with your heart, because there are no orchestras."

"No orchestras? How can this be?"

"You are hearing the pure sound of the composer's spirit, willing and energizing the effusion of music into existence. The melodic concepts are exuding from within each of these exalted prodigies by the sheer power of their visionary enlightenment, forged from Creation's infinite sea of consciousness. *Each artist is the creator and the performer, actualizing their own deepest yearnings.* Every note, every rhythm, and every harmony emerge as a unique tone of truth from the innermost chambers of their pure authentic essence. Inspiration arising from the depths mirrors in performance the exact emotional reflection of heart and soul."

Our guide further emphasizes this vision to us....

"Resonating from deep within the core of the valleys, swirling orchestral colors begin to take shape and form, as sounds intertwine and unite. Unseen choirs resonate elegant sonatas, oratorios, and concertos into existence. At first they sound like finely-tuned waves of vibration as they rise up in layer upon layer. New creations then softly begin to display the ever so delicate outlines through which noble edifices arise. As these fantastic performances play on, palatial mansions are created from the interwoven sound frequencies, elevating towering crescendos and exquisite arpeggios. Breathtaking melodies and harmonies shine as they continue to fashion themselves into crystalline castles of gleaming light. Vibrational frequencies entwine before our eyes in splendor, creating elegant palaces of luminous sound. Arising dramatically, the transcendent music echoes from the very marrow of the sprawling valleys unto the heavens. These works display the heart of the composer's spirit in rapture and brilliance.

"Then in a sudden burst, as the work reaches its climactic crescendo, the Master Composer disappears! Such *disappearances* have become known and appreciated as glorious initiations. These are royal rites of passage to honor our finest, most accomplished Trasarans, as they ascend to the next realm along the eternal path of love's evolution. In the exact moment of their soul's superlative transition, a new gifted Trasaran, ready to create their own grand composition on this journey, comes forth to become the newest maestro, as the exalted music of life plays on."

We must take a moment to drink in and appreciate all we have experienced. Words like *miraculous* pale, compared to what we have just witnessed. These unique and powerful Beings have achieved states of consciousness far more wondrous than any we could have ever dreamed.

THE GIFT

Twin celestial messengers unlike any we've seen, appear instantaneously before our guide. Radiantly glowing, energy lights streaming forth from them, they communicate in a way we can feel, but cannot comprehend. We ponder what this all means.

Then just as the messengers vanish, our guide turns to us, exuding the essence of pure bliss.

All along our journey he has been optimistic, enthusiastic, and jubilant. It is obvious that he takes immense pleasure in showing us his wonderful world as his elation seems magnified many times over. He beams new thoughts to us.

"Guiding the travelers, who have found their way here to experience Trasara and all of its wonders, has always brought us supreme fulfillment and great joy. There was inevitably a place or time along our way, however, when we could venture no further. The witnessing of our most enlightened Trasarans rising through creativity to become transcendent Grand Masters, and then celebrating their passage into the awaiting Globe of White, was as far as most could journey.

"It brings me tremendous delight to impart to you what I have just received. You, dear souls, are to be gifted a rare glimpse into a Trasaran marvel so very few have ever seen. Continued passage has been granted, empowering you to witness one of the most spectacular natural wonders in all Trasara."

We can feel the magnitude of this incomparable honor fill us with profound excitement. Becoming weightless, this presence gently draws us upward and we rise higher and higher above the valleys and the mountaintops. From this new vantage point, stretching out to where the horizon meets the azure skies, we can see in totality the ongoing interactions containing the eternal truths of the entire Trasaran civilization.

At last our view expands even further and the rare sight our guide alluded to is revealed. In stunned rapture, we are silent and filled with awe as our eyes rise to behold the unbelievable. Commanding the entire space over, beyond, and above the sky's horizon, we see endless waters reflecting glistening colors of mother of pearl, flowing out into infinity. *Yes, as impossible as it may seem, we see an Ocean in the Sky!*

THE OPALESCENT SEAS OF TRASARA

We knew the Trasarans had found ways beyond what we once deemed to be the laws of nature, having exceeded many of the limitations that still persist on our world. But this? Now we understand and realize Trasara is free from the bonds of gravity itself. *We are not under the ocean but rather this spectacular ocean is above us, miraculously floating on its own.* In an anomalous contradiction to everything our senses tell us, this massive supernatural body of water covers the space far and wide above the city of Trasara, rushing out to splash on the limitless shores of imagination. Because our eyes were not looking, we could not see. Because our senses labored, mired in limitation consciousness, we were not able to fathom the possibility of a civilization so powerful as to alter the natural phenomena of gravity and create, at will, an extraordinary new inversion of reality.

Now we understand what our guide meant when he said we would be gifted a rare glimpse. Indeed, we did not, we could not conceive or grasp the boundless wonder of Trasara's most magnificent gift. Here, as we gaze upward astonished by the wonderworks of the inexplicable, we are drawn deeper into a transcendence of consciousness surpassing any of our wildest imaginings.

Our guide reflects reverently now...

"You have flowed into a new state of awareness and now your senses can perceive the soaring Opalescent Seas of Trasara. Individuals immersed in their connection with the gleaming waters above are developing wisdom and insight through their own command of the primal creative force. Philosopher-scientists and elevated intellects, geniuses and poets of Universal Mind and thought reside here. The immeasurable immensity of the very ocean is required for these Grand Masters of Consciousness to define and contemplate the never-ending forms of thought and mind. In the expansion of all knowledge in an enduring way, the limitation of what is unquestioned and well accepted is perpetually giving way to the new truths waiting to be awakened and revealed.

"These individuals are working at the most far-reaching heights and depths to exceed what was once thought to be inevitable, static, and immutable. They have discovered that idea and wisdom are also vibrational frequencies and, as such, reside in endless Source Consciousness. Innovators and explorers into Divine Mind are continually inventing and creating new, original, and unique ways to comprehend and interact with the farthest reaches of the uncharted and undiscovered.

"Thoroughly embracing these new and as yet untried methods of envisioning universal wisdom and energy, held by the very oceans themselves, these masters of mind pursue the cutting edge of awareness. In nature, creations of Universal Mind are more tenuous and challenging to realize. Often they are first discovered as misty nebulous abstractions, even otherworldly and beyond description. Each grand explorer of consciousness strives to answer the unanswerable questions, conceive the ultimate solutions, and master the limitations of what lies beyond those abstractions. These are almost timeless endeavors, yet when the moment arrives, they also vanish in a glorious light, signaling departure and transformation into their next evolutionary life expression.

"As these new emergent truths lead us onward, there is an expectant excitement, drawing us into the as yet unknown expansion of what is possible, along our ever-evolving pathway to love. All Trasarans stand in awe of these mysterious and glorious moments. Within each of us is the aspirational awareness and knowing that all will ultimately experience these rapturous transcendent truths over and again."

In this astonishing moment of clarity, we see the sustained essence of each soul displaying the individual affirmations of each prodigy's personal journey into the unknown. Here, the visualized creations of every universal champion of mind become illuminated so all may view, witness, and feel love's most profound revelation of life through this very fusion.

Even though these master mind explorers have transcended these dimensions, their authentic commitment to unifying heart and mind remains. They leave for us the brilliant jewels of love and inspiration, perpetually shining for all to behold. The altruistic reflections that well up from within each of these connected souls bestow deep reverence and vision of this ongoing journey to love.

THOSE BEYOND

Our guide has more to impart to us...

"The Trasaran Cycle of Becoming is a pinnacle experience for all life on our world, yet there is always the awaiting unknown, mysterious, and divine. All along our journey through Trasara, you may have heard whispers of *Those Beyond*. Although it is nearly unimaginable, there is a reality that can only be described as the finest mist of the Opalescent Sea's future spray. It waits on the other side of the grand master's ultimate passage.

"Perpetually striving to move us forward, there are those who exist in every design of life's evolution, constantly blazing the way. It is through Those Beyond that we take our direction. Although we do not know for sure, Trasarans feel it could be the grand masters, having ascended to a state surpassing the White Globe, who have become Those Beyond. They serve as beacons, receiving the most distant emanations of consciousness yet perceived, and in their ecstasy, they shine forth to all.

"From the ones taking their first steps along the path to the most advanced among us, all are forever in touch with those who have arrived at the farthest edge of possibility... *Those Beyond*."

REFLECTIONS

With the exquisiteness of all Trasara spread out before us, glistening in its compelling wonderment, one of us looks toward our guide and sighs, "Your city seems truly perfect in every way."

"Ahh... the only real perfection is Source," adds our guide. "Although we have mastered this level of life, new revelations are always dawning. Perfection is merely a perception, elusive and delicate, and often held for only an instant. Then it's so easily lost."

We are curious to know more. Everything flows and feels so incredibly effortless here, so we ask our guide, "Is there still any challenge left to life?"

"Challenge? Indeed. There is always challenge.

"To surpass what is already known and view what no other has is a never-ending endeavor and our most admirable aspiration. We constantly strive to actualize the soaring yearnings that remain as yet unrealized.

"We delve deeper into the eternal nature of our existence, seeking to reveal the mysteries that will enlighten the course of our evolution. Every challenge, once mastered, carves out and unveils yet another footprint on the path... the path to All.

"We move perpetually toward Source, yet the expanse, both inwardly and outwardly, is so vast. Those Beyond, who are conscious of the still unknown, continue to mark the path of the eternal odyssey so all may travel The Great Way. Yet, at the last, each one must always make their journey into oneness, alone.

"Our city represents a community of personal expression, a way for our entire race to contemplate and identify that which we are. It also allows us the opportunity to discover Creation's deepest reality, which is forever changing, being transformed by the constantly dawning new truth. Trasara provides a vehicle for us to fully realize all that is within the seen and unseen, as we continue to fulfill our vast potential."

Our guide then projects a glorious stream of light revealing the wondrous harmony of all Trasarans working together as One in absolute unity.

Smiling, his continuing message resonates within us... "All Trasarans devote themselves through the act of personal choice and are fully committed to blessing the whole of life through love, beauty, wisdom, and harmony. By embracing this forever-evolving way of life, our entire race is enhanced. Truly, we have come to know the power of life dedicated to abundance for all."

We are filled with a sense of wonder that surpasses all of our former experience, and we say to our guide... "Gazing upon your splendid city, we see and feel your consummate dedication to the pursuit of life's most authentic embodiment of true prosperity. Witnessing the Divine Essence within, realizing its Source, we can now experience this prosperity as it transforms itself into love. The pure exhilaration that resides here is so beautiful."

MAGNIFICENCE AWAITS

Our guide continues softly now... "As splendid as our city is, there is an entire universe that lies before you. It is teeming with endless varieties of life, all striving for perfection within the scope of their own evolution. Traveling along The Great Way, we have achieved this miraculous moment, this mystical milestone of Now. Yet, as you have seen, through holding fast to our unwavering faith, we are ever striving to expand our awareness founded on the truth of transcendence through creativity. If you choose to continue onward, you will most assuredly encounter evolutionary dimensions that far outshine the epiphanies you have beheld on Trasara. The degree of perfection and truth that all life can attain is never ending and boundless, as we all strive to become one with the unimaginable possibilities.

"Countless multitudes came before us, and infinite masses have evolved into dimensions unknown, creating far more profound realities than even we can fathom or embrace. Source is wondrous, seemingly magical, and as our spirits unfold, Source instills in us a deep unquenchable desire to find our way home.

"In your continuing quest, you may even come to experience future encounters with Those Beyond."

"Unlimited magnificence awaits. "This is why you have been guided here, to see and experience the sights and sounds of Transcendent Consciousness itself, lifting you onward.

"We know the path ahead will lead you to the awakening of your grandest truth. In parting, we wish you boundless inspiration and blessings along your journey."

Our guide begins to beam with effusive colors so brilliant and bright that he becomes too radiant to look upon. We turn away for but an instant, yet when our gaze returns... he is gone!

COSMIC CONSCIOUSNESS

Chapter Three

UNIVERSE OF UNIVERSES

HIGHER AND DEEPER

Although the threshold of the cosmic beckons us, we cannot just step across. Our hearts must first attune to the elevated emotions that mirror this deeply profound vibrational frequency of consciousness. Let us take a moment to pause.... This journey is not just a matter of walking up steps, as the steps will only become plateaus. Preparing ourselves in advance is essential, for this quest can only resume when an enlightened shift of conscious emotional clarity occurs.

From here, gazing outward into the universe, we are but a small droplet in a ceaseless eternal ocean, appearing to be lost in the unimaginable immensity of the vast unknown. Yet, in this same incomparable instant, if we go within and feel the all-encompassing love that is us, we will know with perfect certainty that we are One with all.

Suspended in an inner space where there is no motion, strive now to *will* your heart and mind into a singular vision of Love's awareness. This is where every soul must ask the daunting question... *"Am I ready to face and dissolve the barriers that prevent me from ascending further?"* Each soul can choose to embrace the actuality of their personal life endeavors and elevate beyond everything that is not their authentic self, or turn away to wait again for another opportunity. The path to shedding these self-illusions is simple, but simple does not mean easy.

Focusing inward, recall the special occasions when you were touched and transformed by the pure act of loving. Search for the special times you felt this most passionate or joyous of life's experience. Being fully present in the moment, bring forth your greatest memories of love. Blending your highest awareness with love's magnificence, unite them as One. Allow these emotions to focus your essence, infusing your spirit with bliss-filled remembrance, as your heart opens to what lies ahead.

Be aware that in recalling these elevated visions of love, you may have to confront subtler, hidden elements. These are the outer layers of personality, steadily fashioned over a lifetime, which can obscure the awareness of your soul's true essence. Often these layers or traits are so familiar, so close, their reflections project a false sense of self, obscuring who you really are. Going further now, explore the sweeping fullness of your own inner universe.

While contemplating your life's evolving drama, hold fast to the authentic truth of your vision of love. From this expanded perspective you will clearly see the dynamics of the blinding captivations that flowed from the outer world. This unveiled perception of higher vision fused with love, exposes life's deceptions and unmasks the illusions that influenced you so completely, so persuasively, in their efforts to make you believe they were your reality.

As these mesmerizing impressions unfolded, perhaps they convinced you they were genuine. Trusting in the outside world, with its people, possessions, and the busy repetitions of day-to-day existence, it was easy to believe this held the true meaning of life. Without the ability to discern that these impressions were merely alluring appearances, you may have ultimately designed your existence around them. Thus, your direction was forged and set into motion. Making decisions and choices based on judgments formulated from a reality you possibly came to believe was undeniable, distracted you from your inherent nature, your singular source of essence.

Time continued onward as your soul developed and tried to contend with the outward swirl of the hypnotic dance, clouding the connection to your authentic self. These distractions caused the sight of your innate spirit to grow dim, ultimately fading from view.

Looking inward you can pull back the layers and sheaths of those once accepted false beliefs, revealing the hidden textures of human emotion. From clashing with your most fearsome rivals, to seeking the full passion of your greatest loves, these compelling feelings bestowed a sense of importance to your life. All the agonies and ecstasies, victories and defeats, had powerful effects to be sure. Through the intricacies of ambition and desire, this continuous drama deeply molded and shaped your reality.

In this moment of unblemished reflection, you are met with a clear vision of truth and the most bewildering of questions may surface. *Why did I make those decisions? What was I searching for? Why did the judgement of others affect me so?* To see and simply cast off the false illusions of those sophisticated conclusions you once accepted as your reality, while still holding true to the deepest love born in your original heart's desire, is one of the greatest challenges to attaining enlightenment.

Take strength in knowing that many of us have experienced similar deceptions in our own lives. We have also been caught up in the incessant chatter and glowing enticements of what so often came to be seen as our own false reality. You are not alone!

Even when our actions are wrapped in the sincerest of intentions, if they are based on a distorted sense of self, the path ultimately leads to emptiness and disappointment. *This is the outer world of life's illusion known as Maya.*

Outer events, no matter how genuine they seemed, were never real. They only seemed real because we mistakenly placed our value and meaning of existence in them, naively surrendering our trust and belief to these fleeting illusions of life's empty circus.

Our perfect essence has always been buried and waiting, submerged beneath this collective state of amnesia. Like a pearl, we have been asleep, concealed in our shell, yet growing ever more beautiful until we fully awaken and our open heart crosses the threshold into a new state of awareness. No longer obscured by misty misconceptions, our inner light is freed and burns bright, springing forth into consciousness. *At last we recognize the Eye that is I.*

Being able to distinguish between the truth of love and the shedding of our false attachments, we can ascend into higher dimensions, where awaits the crowning breakthrough of becoming unified with all.

Not until we arise as our own illuminated presence, can the illusions once thought to be reality, dissipate. Life and spirit are then beautifully transformed from within the radiant Source of Love.

Often, in the midst of awakening, we struggle to understand why? Why has this happened? How did we forget? Although we might never fully know the answers to these questions, we can ultimately learn from the essential nature of our challenging journey. This learning brings with it new vision and the joyous realization that had it not been for the unseen influences in each of our encounters, we would have never grown into this present instant, this pinnacle of awakening. Everything that has ever happened to us had purpose and value, because it brought us closer to remembering our true self.

Our spirit has never been concerned about the passage of time or our chosen path of growth, but rather it has lovingly waited, knowing we would ultimately find our way. Enlightenment has forever been about the quality of our life's journey, not the *how* of it or *when* we would arrive.

In our full awakening, the mists of misperception are fully vanquished and life's truth becomes crystal clear.

We are filled with a joy beyond measure, yet in this quiet stillness it can be challenging to accept that the meaning of the joys and tears that have affected our lives so deeply only felt real because we slowly came to believe in our own judgments, myths, and fables. Now, through this supreme breakthrough of clarity and love, we can bravely confront and expose our misleading beliefs and falsehoods. Releasing the outer world of ubiquitous deception and seeing beyond the masks of our own self-illusion takes great courage, but here the opportunity of attaining elevated consciousness shines bright with unwavering inspiration.

Go within to your sacred space and visit a time when purest love enveloped and poured forth from you, beaming throughout your entire life. The splendor of these experiences is imprinted forever in your soul. Focus on one of these memories of love and hold fast until you feel it shining. You can be certain love is there, because love is the source of your creation. These are the very definitions of the grandest horizons, deepest valleys and most glorious vistas of the breathtaking adventure that is your *authentic life*. Precious, rare, and revered, these moments embody the most genuine treasures your heart will always remember.

With sights set upward, wholly immersed in the bliss of spirit, set your soul free inspiring its innermost flood of emotion to embrace your deepest passion, tenderness and devotion. Feeling the most glorious love you've ever known, seek to thoroughly realize the fullness of your totality. Awaken and feel creation's greatest gift. As you do, love will etherealize before you and blossom from within. Love's eternal presence merging with the shimmering memories of that most beloved jewel no longer buried within will carry you onward and upward.

Through these realizations, we come to feel the deepest gratitude, admiration, and respect for all that has happened. In reviewing the events of life, profound feelings of compassion, empathy, and loving appreciation come forth, for at last we know our raison d'etre, our reason for being. We can truly honor each event with respect and acceptance as a genuinely necessary and relevant element of life.

We experience these insights, as seen through the truth of our Inner Eye, as epiphanies that define the difference between merely existing and living absolutely from the loving soul power of Source Creation. Each and every experience illuminating our undiscovered path echoed like a soft voice, calling to us. Now, the mystery is solved, and in sparkling light we can see that all the while, life was guiding us home to the boundless Love of Source.

Continuously rising into new dimensions of the here and now, we become increasingly aware that our soul is reintegrating, becoming one with the cresting wave of our original spark of life.

Within each of us dwells our authentic living essence.

This is what beats our heart, breathes our breath, and gives us the gift of life. Before enlightenment, we unknowingly gave and received this priceless gift, wrapped in the false allure of the outer world. When looking through awakened eyes, the once promised gleam of the world *out there,* wanes in its allure, and is shown to be only the playground of unfulfilled promises. Embracing the knowledge that we are now on the road to transformational awakening, our decisions are seen as pathways of destiny, designed to bring the deepest awareness of our soul light to the surface.

In its emergence through our heart, the light of understanding shines forth, and we see that while searching for the meaning of life out there, The Truth has always been right here, within us. What we have been looking for… is what is looking. Now we can see that the "outside in" awareness was never real, because it is the "inside out" expression of our eternal nature that radiates into life from our inner essence. Reaching for itself through us, the gift of life energizes the ever-expanding radiance of our enlightenment. This is the secret and the origin of our creation. Through becoming one with the realizer of these experiences, duality dissolves into that pure Presence of absolute love.

Ever seeking greater and more unique ways to know Itself, Source explores this gift of life as us, fulfilling a ceaseless yearning to unconditionally love all of Creation. Source is that Presence forever calling from our true self.

Rise up! Let us cast off the illusion of what we once thought certain, for the time has arrived to leave past limitations behind and step through the doors of unending possibility. Our divine soul shines as we wondrously blossom into our innate brilliancy of fully awakened Beings.

Originating from beyond our consciousness, a fascinating anticipation emerges. Do you feel it drawing us upward and into the cosmic expanse of our universe? In total exhilaration, fully acquiescing to this emotional tide with transformed vision and expanded hearts, we are ready to embrace the next great chapter of our continuing journey into consciousness. Come!

THE MIGHTY ANGEL

As the space around us begins to swirl, we see a portal open as beams of radiant light come flying through. The portal becomes larger and larger, vibrating into a torus field filled with colors of incredible beauty. Streaming forth from the center of this field of light, a glorious angel appears. In his right outstretched palm rests a large gleaming orb, ablaze and aglow with the luminosity of a million suns. The look on his face is one of great jubilation and utter devotion. In this same instant, we sense he knows exactly what we are feeling. His message resonates within us, and although unspoken, we understand completely.

"You are about to rise and become expanding beacons of elevated awareness, awakened and revealed. Let this realization burst within you. You will come to know beyond any doubt that truth and love are unlimited in grandeur as they spiral on into eternity. The hour is upon you to soar to a new dimension beyond the conditions of your lives, delivering you to the spectacular realms that await your arrival.

"Each of you has the power to embrace your deepest self. Your heart merely needs to feel love to release this shining beauty from within you. Allow the walls holding this gift captive to crumble. Grant your heart the freedom to be touched, revealing your own wisdom and desire. Empower your essence to mirror that One True Essence. Your happiness will increase beyond any measure as you see, feel, and understand that all hearts resonate with the same shine and shimmer of Universal Oneness.

"Perfect love flows through every heart. This is the bond that will always draw us together. At last you will understand you are pure spirit and love. This is the eternal spring through which all life flows. Enter this sacred space of love within you, for it is from this place the next phase of your ascension will begin.

"The ability to see the flow of love, grace, and beauty emanating from your heart can often be elusive. Perhaps you know it as your ultimate good, or an inner place of quiet. Each of us has this sanctuary of peace and tranquility within. Let us go to this cherished space now, so you can rise to the next heartfelt awakening of your journey. Behold, the wonders that await you!

In a grand gesture his left arm sweeps upward, and pure light pours from his outstretched hand. Pointing above, the portal becomes larger and larger, opening up to the very heavens themselves, and there before us lies the limitless cosmos.

The space behind us becomes faint as into the deep we rise....

THE MILKY WAY AND BEYOND

Our sights become star-bound as effortlessly we glide past the layers of Terra into space.

Our sun radiates in golden splendor, but soon becomes lost in a billion specks of light as we ascend through the dark center of the Milky Way.

The boundless universe expands before us, and we see in one breathtaking vision that all of its processes are visible and alive as a single creative Being.

Spiral and elliptical galaxies of such grandeur fly before us, each possessing their own incomparable scheme of creation. Arrayed in stunning star-cloaks, each proclaims their ultimate identity. Other more abstract clouds appear and then fade amid fiery nebulae taking shape as we witness new galaxies being born in startling beauty.

Let us pause to listen....

Radiating from each planet, each star, each cluster, and every galaxy, we hear the sound of its individuality, its own vibrational pulse. The planets combine to strike the chord of their own particular solar systems. These melodies unite with the roar of the stars to form the multitude of vibrational colors emanating from each galaxy. Then, in one stupendous masterpiece, the galaxies join together to play the cosmic symphony of the

Universe of Life. This sublime ecstasy is the Music of the Spheres, The Primordial Om. These are the sounds of the vibrational frequencies of all creations, past, present, future, and eternal, simultaneously resonating as One. The actuality of our comprehension is but a whisper, compared to what we are seeing. But oh! What a spectacular sight!

The galaxies are like exalted artists, performing their roles in the universal scheme, acting and reacting upon one another, with the mysterious darkness of space as their stage. Dancing across the waves of vibrational frequencies flowing from them, each moves to the will and intention of the unfathomable script.

Continuing onward the furious energy beacons of the quasars, the powerful searchlights of the universe, come into view. They are but pinpoints within massive auras, extending monumental amounts of energy to all they touch. What majesty they emanate! They shine more brightly than a thousand galaxies!

There are grand cycles in the process of unfolding, as the star-swirls seek the infinite reaches of space in order to grow into their future fullness. Shaped and fashioned by idea and energy, their supreme identities are reflected and woven into creation's cosmic masterpiece. Even our ability to hear has been expanded and enhanced, and we remain motionless, momentarily entranced by the sheer brilliance we view.

Ahead of us dawns the edge of our universe. Approaching the last outpost, incredible as it may seem, before us we see the horizon line, the line of light. *This line is likened to a waterfall that does not go down but rather out in all directions.* Approaching, we feel powerfully attracted, irresistibly drawn into the ineffable and unexplored.

Pausing briefly in loving admiration and gratitude, we behold the magnificence of our home universe, and then onward we fly without delay into the supreme mysteries that await.

Moving closer to the waterfall of light, we allow ourselves to be pulled into the waves and are gently cast through the subtle line separating our universe, until... There, do you see it? Do you see the fountain?

THE FOUNTAIN

Having journeyed past the boundaries of our universe, we glance back over the tremendous distance we have just traversed, drinking in the totality of our home universe and its infinite celestial wonders. What we view is remarkable, for now we comprehend that these accumulated marvels are happening within a *collected* area of space, not our space, but *another*. What we thought was a continuous and seemingly unending universe with its countless creations, exists fully within an area shaped like an immense transparent sphere. The sum total of all its starry creations is embodied within, never spilling past or beyond these unseen boundaries. *It is like looking at an image being projected into a sphere, and then having the sphere disappear, yet the image remains.*

Beaming from its center, the stars of our home world shine in a continuous expansion of infinite stellar horizons. Beautiful omnidirectional waves of light swell and their dazzling sprays of spiral coloration appear to be reaching out beyond the boundaries of the invisible sphere seeking this spectacular new realm. Completely surrounding our home universe, this newly discovered dimension is very present and highly-charged, yet it looks finer, more delicate, and appears to extend beyond infinity. As fantastic as this is, the most breathtaking sight is the fountain!

Welling up from within, flowing over and continually spilling down the sides of our sphere of star creations, a magnificent fountain is distinctly visible. The liquid light pouring from the fountain provides an endless source of nourishment to our universe. Somehow, we feel this flow is the animating force through which all life, as we know it, draws its very existence.

Projecting a gleaming luminosity, the fountain's glowing colors continually shift and change as they ray out across this new dimension.

Shining in glory before us, we innately intuit that this wellspring is merely a symbol of the Mighty Being that animates our evolution. Nurturing the lives of the countless creations within its charge, this flow perpetually pours out to each and all. We feel the pure intention of this Grand Being in a sheer ecstasy and divine love, and a longing to uphold the creations it has chosen to shepherd.

We see other, similar lights far in the distance. They are luminescent and aglow. *Can there be countless universes in an eternity beyond any knowing?* Our vision shows us they are there, yet these mysterious universes appear incomprehensible to us, as they develop exclusive evolutionary forces within their own individual schemes of never-ending possibility.

Contemplating this moment with reverence, the vastness of our view is both captivating and enchanting.

These illustrious Beings form a grand universe of immortals so breathtaking in their magnificence that they soar beyond any mere concept of gods. Yet, as incredible as it may seem, we can sense that they are also evolving, seeking to become more fully aware of whence they came. Forever attuned with Source, expressing their own unique energies within infinite consciousness, these Beings ultimately defy the most far-reaching perception of what we consider exalted ones.

Our sight comes to rest, centering into a panoramic view, beaming brightly to the far distant edges of this new dimension. Even this degree of awareness, however, does not mean the vastness of the infinite reaches of space is fully visible to us. *If it were possible to travel beyond all boundaries, there would always and forever be a limitless horizon.*

There is so much that remains unseen, yet looking closer, our perception shows us an even grander, seemingly unfathomable depth to ponder. All the dazzling streaming galaxies and the entirety of the countless space conceptions are only made visible against the backdrop of the dark unknown space by which all creations of light are expanding through and across. Neither empty nor a void, this darkness feels to be brimming with energy and most certainly contains countless yet undiscovered realms. This is the limited reflection of an infinite eternity that is absolutely beyond the discernment of any finite mind.

The presence of this mystifying complexity is so vast that we are simply unable to distinguish its true nature. We can only call it *darkness* because we do not have the language or awareness to fully encompass these as yet inconceivable elements of creation. Even though we know this darkness is highly charged with energy, there will never be an idea, a thought, or a rationale that will grant us even a minute glint of what lies in or beyond it. Any portrayal of life from this unqualified darkness would most certainly be so completely foreign to us, that we could not grasp its laws of existence, or even that it exists at all!

Understanding and comprehension are concepts that drive us, yet they are not the means whereby this eternally boundless phenomena can ever be known. Were it possible to conceive both the dark and the light in their entirety this revelation would still be but a single grain of sand on an endless beach of another forever.

WHO IS LOOKING?

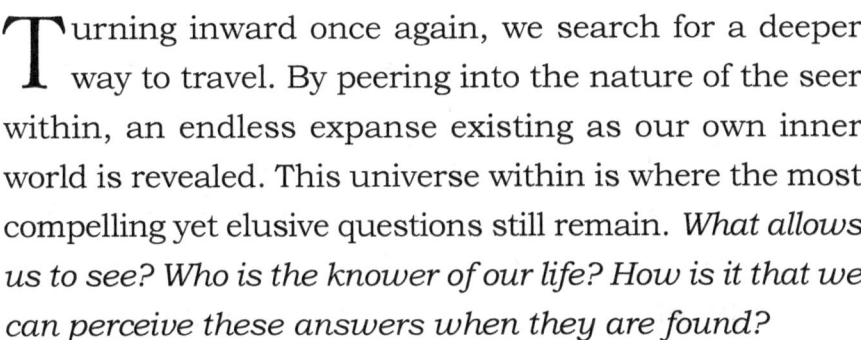

Turning inward once again, we search for a deeper way to travel. By peering into the nature of the seer within, an endless expanse existing as our own inner world is revealed. This universe within is where the most compelling yet elusive questions still remain. *What allows us to see? Who is the knower of our life? How is it that we can perceive these answers when they are found?*

Plumbing the depths of our essence, we still feel a sense of duality. We are seeking an arcane and mysterious initiation of awareness. At our conception we became a new instrument of perception. In that instant the gift of becoming our own observer was bestowed on us. That oneness of sight flowing from our inner point of perception is the witness of our very existence, yet it remains a pure reflection of the infinite observer of all. In this manner, we are both individuality and infinite universality. While searching for our true self, the paradox is that we are actually searching for *that* which we already are!

We have already dispelled the many reflections of life's distractions and deceptions that blurred our vision. In truth there is only one steady shining stream of never-ending brilliance that has been made known. Our journey began in multiplicity, and through our growth the once hidden masks concealing our inborn identity dissolved and we became our own ever-present Higher Self.

In our passion to proceed, we must wholeheartedly embrace our inherent authenticity as a singular creative expression of life. The desire to achieve deeper awareness compels us to travel roads that narrow with each new awakening, as the pathways leading to our most authentic self become even finer. Making more courageous choices, we are elevated to new levels of effectiveness, granting each of us the gifts of transformative breakthroughs. Through this transcendence and beyond the stormy seas of everyday life, our personal reality emerges and basks in the waves of newfound love.

The birthright of all living beings is the expression of our inner Light as our true self. The nature of our quest is to become powerful beacons, illuminating the ocean of unlimited love. Through seeking to fulfill this greatest desire to know ourselves, we discover that which opens us fully to unity with Source. This is the gift by which we can explore the extraordinary landscape of our own immortality. To awaken completely, is to experience life from beyond the senses. Having banished and dissolved lifetimes of superficial judgments, we are now on the path that unveils our inner light. It is a seeming contradiction, but true nonetheless, that as we progress backward into the Light of our conception, we are also moving forward into that very same revelation. No longer imprisoned by the guise of mythical delusion, the webs of our own confusion have fallen away, one-by-one. Ever more scintillating we shine, brighter than any imagining, continually reaching out and striving to once again renew our original radiant awareness. By unmasking and illuminating our fathomless depths, we become the light-vision-awareness of our revealed reality.

We have lifted the finest self-woven veils of misjudgment that once distorted and obscured our vision, and we can clearly see that pure essence of life, that constant Presence, is our Source created self. This pure self is the grand observer that has witnessed every breath of every moment without judgment.

In retrospect, we fully recognize that every past memory we recall is from the perspective of *Now*. Standing strongly in the present, it becomes ever clearer, that even when we consider tomorrow and beyond, the future can only be imagined from where and who we are in the present moment. Our most expansive connection and deepest realization are only possible when at last we come to rest in oneness with the eternal *Now*. This is where duality disappears. *Now, is pure Consciousness, the home of our soul, and the only truth of being.* This infinite state of Presence has been given countless names... Nirvana... Samadhi... Paradise... It has even been called... *Heaven.*

Progressing inward to view our luminous origins, we have expanded to beam even brighter still. Shining out from the depths of all and revealing what was once hidden has been our way to enlightenment. The fullness expressed so effortlessly is Source, flowing with grace and ease from within us. In arriving at this realization, we understand that the end and the beginning are one and the same.

Higher and deeper, as an example, is not a mental concept or a spatial designation. Even though we use descriptive directions such as outward and inward, upward and downward, in reality there are no directions. There is only a singular totality of self-realization as it reaches for oneness with All. The desire to know ourselves more fully is a multidimensional pursuit representing our yearning to become an instrument of creation and discovery. *Diving deeper means to love absolutely. Reaching higher means fully embracing The Light.* With each successive breakthrough, our unique gifts and soul qualities expand simultaneously, merging with our transformational spirit and forging a deeper bond with all life. Once known, this soul awareness is forever ours and can never again be lost or forgotten.

When our essence is fully freed, it shines into the entirety of all life, emanating the luminescence it has always been. With each new awakening, we grow into the fullness of our empowered cosmic self. We ultimately continue to express the light of the Divine. Source Love grows us with each successive stage of our enlightenment, and like a flower naturally knows to reach for the sun, we forever strive to know the sun within our own heart.

Refining the ability to become who we truly are within the vast ocean of awareness holds the key to the eternal path that unlocks the door to infinite awareness. In knowing there is only the brilliance of The Light seeking and finding the radiance of Source. Our journey becomes a joyous revelation as our new transcendent and elevated awareness awakens us to who we truly are.

Leaving behind any concept of time and space, our soul-force energizes us firmly into the Now. When we embrace with absolute knowing, that our own heartbeat is one with every galaxy and every particle, from the grandest to the smallest, this is when we fully attune in unity with Cosmic Consciousness.

Willfully allowing the joyful light of Source to effortlessly pass through us without restraint complements our soaring spirit, and life's flow is imbued with the ecstasy of the highest states of awareness. Through this ecstasy, our will aligns our soul with the waves of Source Will, restoring equilibrium and a balanced state of eternal bliss.

Moving beyond mere thoughts and concepts of love, past all limitation both real and imagined, we experience the deepest point of stillness within. But our ultimate journey of awakening does not end here. Once our total light *is* a pure reflection of the One Great Light... *This is where the true journey begins!*

IS THERE NO END

Refocusing our vision once again at the edge of the farthest reaches of space, the immense cosmos we have traversed shines before us. In our unceasing desire to continue on, our awareness has been amplified and magnified exponentially, as once again we illuminate the heights and depths of our total awareness. Having discovered the shining gleam of that far greater illumination, we are ready to proceed.

Many, however, will come to a barrier of overwhelming frustration at this phase of the journey. Looking out at a seemingly boundless expanse, doubt may arise. There will still be those who must, in their own hearts, ask questions. *Is there no end? Does each dimension give way to yet another, reaching always to the next? Must we simply continue on, embracing each new dimension, never reaching a final destination?* These questions and countless others, seem to resound beyond all knowing. How will it be possible to conceive this vastness?

SPIRIT DAUGHTER

Out of the darkness emanating from the surrounding space, a sparkling swirl of light begins to move toward us. With each dazzling step, we feel something magnificent is about to happen, until in a mysterious way we never dreamed possible, a beautiful spiritual presence suddenly materializes before us. In this moment, we are suspended and spellbound, for this Being is literally the most exquisite presence we have ever beheld.

Our eyes rise as slowly we drink in the transcendent wonder of her spiritual divinity. Somehow, time stands still, all is motionless, and we are hopelessly entranced by the extraordinary loveliness and delicate power of the celestial Being shimmering in our sight.

Her features are clearly visible, created by the sheerest glowing lines that only subtly and softly portray an image. The transcendent aura of effusive vibrancy pouring from the very center of her heart takes our breath away. Her radiance flows forth, completely filling the entire horizon with the most exquisite brilliance. Exhilarated beyond imagination, our hearts can only wonder... *Where do extraordinary Beings such as these come from?* The awe-inspiring creative power of Source is vast, yet clearly, we can see that every creation is loved so dearly that when the necessity arises, a way forward is always made known.

Shining out in all directions from her heart center, Source Love emanates colors so overwhelmingly effusive that we cannot see beyond or even feel our way through. She smiles, and the beauty of her presence elevates our experience, surpassing what has until now been our highest joy. At last, we are once again able to embody a single thought. Finding our voice, we ask... *Who are you?* In majesty and splendor, her voice resonates within our consciousness, flowing like a song:

"I am a Daughter of Love, rayed out to be with you from the heart of the Universal Mother. We are sent throughout all eternity to help those seekers such as you along the great way. You are on a journey that can take you to your dreams. But I must tell you, realizing the actuality of your dreams does not lie in attempting to comprehend the ultimate nature of the cosmos. This can never be accomplished by the most exalted of Beings, or even by those such as I, who come from realms beyond the infinite. These are endless worlds, existing far past those of the angelic, yet still, the cosmic totality remains forever the eternal mystery.

"Through the compassion and love of the Universal Mother, who cares for all seekers and travelers, I have been sent to assist you with the seriousness of your questions. Let me show you the crossroads where you stand and which path will take you forward in fulfilling your true heart's desire."

She motions for us to move closer and, at first, her illumination commands all in view. Blinded by her splendor, we are unsure what she is trying to disclose. To us, there is only the limitless space that existed before her arrival. We are drawn toward her and into the light surrounding her heart. Just then, the emanation of her image shifts into an entirely new frequency wave and what was once hidden is unmistakably clear. A glorious vison has been opened for us to see and know. What was merely a dark backdrop filled with stars, galaxies, and the Universe of Universes, has been transformed to reveal the very workings of all creation!

SCENES OF CREATION

We see before us what can only be described as a boundless energy expanse, infinitely stretching out to an unseen horizon. Our surroundings are filled with sights, sounds, and emotions that are at once thunderous, yet so incredibly tender. There are innumerable tone tapestries expressing intermingling, glistening, shimmering pillars of sound. Rivers emulating these energy waves swell together and then splash apart, cresting and descending back and forth on one another as they flow onto the shoreless ocean of creation. Profound harmonies of beauty and complexity are created, merging and dancing together for what is only a flashing moment and then instantly parting. The sounds of these exquisite energies appear to be moving toward resolution yet somehow never do. But the most astounding sight is the invisible point that gleams from the very center of our perception.

THE INVISIBLE CENTER

Images of fantastic creations flow from an invisible center on rays of rare energy currents. Streaming into life and continuously emulating one another in melody and motion, new combinations of vibrational sound energies mixed with light are perpetually improvising their richness anew. Absorbing our experience entirely we intuitively drink in these wonders taking form, as they are emanated into existence from this mystical unseen center. Upon bestowal of unique identity, we see that all creations must first pass through this primordial infusion bath of resonant energy.

The initial expressions are vague, somewhat nebulous cloud-like shapes that become clearer and more present as they expand further away from the center. Images of immense Beings fly before us, and entire universes appear to be soaring past, signifying monumental cycles of growth and evolution set into motion. From here, unfolding in this very instant the genesis of these creations is revealed, not in the eternity it will take to expand into their fullness of creative evolution.

The creations manifesting into our view look to be transparent and amazingly pristine, at first. Yet as they reach the primordial fields of sound and ever-changing frequency, a reaction occurs. Here they are bathed in color and vibratory substance, as each individual identity is imbued with its own unique life force through this cosmic process.

All creations are an outpouring of Source. *The invisible center is the symbol through which Source has chosen to reveal itself.* Contained within the master plan of each emanation, there are Beings of all origins who will ultimately be granted the spark of life. All that existed as merely pure potential will be identity-fused within the original scheme of its divine conception, ultimately striving to become perfected instruments of life's transcendent evolution.

Through the gentle pull of a subtle new force, Universal Gravitation makes itself felt here. Everything from Source must be touched and embraced, molded, moved, and shaped into the ultimate destiny of its divinely conceived identity. Gravity works its magic primarily through the fields of vibration, adding substance to all that becomes creation. The Grand Plan conceived by Source is emanated into existence and bestowed with substance through Universal Gravitation.

Again, the Daughter of Love delicately shifts her energy and a beautiful double spiral with the finest multicolored strands of connected living light enfold and lift us directly into the imperceptible center of All.

Simultaneously, every dimension thus far experienced and any that await birth are shone to us, revealing the most elementary and yet the most complex of creation. *Every being, every design of the eternal expression of all life, takes its gift of awareness from this sea of absolute consciousness.* What we are viewing is the crest of creation washing through the eternal Presence of Now. Directed by an unseen hand, all life emerges unceasingly and unfolds through a boundless infinity.

The simple yet perfect truth is that the origin of all existence and its infinite possibilities is a singular emanation. All destinations or eternities, and thus all realities, are merely aspects of One Origin. This is the infinite eternity called *Life*, occurring in a synchronicity that is instantaneous and contemporaneous with all realities... known and unknown!

BEYOND IDEAS—THE SECRET OF CREATION—THE PYRAMID OF PRESENCE

We continue to feel, ever so faintly, the Daughter of Love etherealize around us, as if to strengthen and uphold our ability to be fully present with these miraculous sights. Without her effortless power to bridge the intensity of this experience, we would be overcome and totally disappear. Paramount to our perception, the Daughter of Love has been the divine reflection through which we can glimpse but the slightest perception of these grand realizations. Her rays glisten anew and we are bestowed and infused with a final crowning crescendo of enlightenment.

The Daughter of Love glows in all her glory, and we feel ourselves becoming her heart light. Realizing we have risen to the quintessence of our potential she inspires us to see the one last and uncompromising truth of our existence. Even this glorious Being is challenged to envision this totality, as communication in all its many forms fades in the face of infinity. Yet somehow, she resonates this knowing in our hearts.

We have already seen the most astonishing of revelations. The vast diversity of all we have viewed along our journey springs forth from a singular simplicity.

Now, as our surroundings soften, Source transforms from its original symbol of an Invisible Point into a Pyramid of Light, radiating every possibility of color and frequency into all dimensions. This is the most supreme representation of Source we can comprehend at this stage of our awakening.

Likened to a three-sided pyramid, showing us a glimpse of its divine nature, Source is a singularity expressing three facets of one unity.

SOURCE is the Creator and giver of life, immeasurable, unknowable, and incomprehensible. Through Source flows the origination and bestowal of all identity. Source creates every individual frequency signature of all manifestations and knows every creation it has ever blessed with the unmatched gift of Its love and life. This is the *who* of anything and nothing, happening and non-happening. Without beginning or end, Source is *omnipotent*.

CONSCIOUSNESS represents every potential and contains all conceptions and events, expressed and unexpressed, finite and infinite, eternal and beyond, into everything that has, is, and will ever manifest. The mysterious waves of gravity find their home within this ultimate domain. With maternal tenderness, Consciousness embraces Source Love for all realities great and small. This is the *what* of any-thing and non-thing. Consciousness is *omniscient*.

BEING is pure potentiality. Any action emanated by the loving will of Source, actuates Consciousness to know Its emanations and designates gravity to move this potential into motion. This is the cradle where ideas are born and bestowed with substance, whether they are manifested or pre-expressed. Containing within itself the capacity of unlimited existence –past, present, future, and eternal—Being becomes the resultant reality of Source and Consciousness. This is the *how* of any-thing and no-thing. Being is *omnipresent.*

PRESENCE
THE CHILD OF THREE

PRESENCE is the consummation of the phenomenon of Source, Consciousness and Being, as perceived by all life in all realities and all universes. Presence is the sum total and the fabric upon which every creation of possibility has been, or ever will be woven into becoming. This is the origin or resultant point where any unique genesis of life emerges. Presence is the *where* of any-thing and no-thing. It is apparently omnipresent, but only as a revelation of the three-fold reality of Source. Should it come to pass that Source would choose to will itself into a new manifestation of existence it would most certainly bring about a new and unique transformation of Presence.

Responsive to the frequencies emanated upon and from within it, Presence eternally retains the imprint of all desire, cause, and identity. From the smallest micro particle to the grandest super universe, it continues the advancement and flourishing of the relationships and interrelationships of all energy and every expression of life. Presence is the ultimate loom on which Source, Consciousness, and Being weave the fabric of all Creation.

The initial superstructures we viewed streaming past us were given identity, and then set into motion by Source through its constant interaction with Consciousness, as the ever-evolving energy of idea created unique living architecture in Being. Even though all conceptions form countless myriads of combinations within themselves, each creation retains its authentic design, its unique frequency signature. The originality and totality of all individual identity is gravitationally held in the Presence of Now as its energy is continually redrawn into the next creation of life. The interaction of the "Three as One," animates the dimensions and supreme realities of all that is known and unknown.

What a glory to behold. Being, completely reflects in Presence the intimate interactions between Source and Consciousness. Presence is the incomprehensible totality receiving the stabilizing impulses from Consciousness, as it spirals through gravity to manifest as the bestowal of Source. Presence becomes, in every conceivable manner, the table upon which the Feast of Life is set.

FROM THE GREATEST TO THE LEAST

Through this design Source has ensured that each and every life, from the greatest to the least, is provided with choice and free will to design its own quality of existence, either knowingly or unknowingly, through the flow of their own vibrational signatures. All vibrational action will energize a reaction into Presence.

Focusing through our personal strength of spirit-will, our life energy radiates into this perpetual now, first to conceive a body of expression, then continuing to have a living impact upon whatever dimension in which we choose to dwell. The secret of living and loving to the fullest lies in transcending the closed system of effects and mono-dimensional identification. This is accomplished through mastering heartfelt creativity, the highest state of cause itself and the key to becoming the oneness of our pure and loving originality.

Infused with identity from Source, as meta-celestial Beings of essence, we are each distinguishable within the sea of infinite Presence. Miraculously, each of us has our own unique vibrational signature, and thus we can experience whatever realm we are capable of attuning to.

When our personal life actions are initiated from this state of awareness, they emerge and resonate, flowing freely and directly as One Presence. By externalizing the quality of who we are and what we envision, willful creativity grants us the ability to spiritize our own uniqueness into vibratory expression. As our inner gifts of vision and love shine into our living reality, our mirrored reflection is always an exact match to our essence in Presence!

Living a life that perfectly reflects our own inner perception and desire is assured when our heart sets the course and our spirit lights the way. This is the original meaning of "as above, so below."

Can this be? Can the infinitude of the vast multiplicity we have viewed ultimately be formed of such a profound yet simple action? Is ALL that IS, purely the combined actions of Source informing Consciousness to emanate into Being what is to become Presence? The answers, lying there before us, are elegant and undeniable in their grandeur.

Yet, immersed in this moment of ultimate reverence and even as great as these insights are, we are overwhelmed when we realize the grandeur of our view is merely a reflective shadow of what is truly the greatest reality, the unfathomable Source....

Ever so faintly, the face of the Daughter of Love begins to reappear, with light pouring from her pure, radiant heart center through which these perceptions have been made possible. We are entranced and enraptured beyond measure. It took a benevolent Being of this magnitude to expand the limitations of our awareness and grant us the ability to grasp the deepest meaning of these resplendent visions. *Now, at last, through our hearts, we once again feel her song....*

"When first we met, you sought to know if the universe is endless? The answer to your question is a resounding, yes! Even the most exalted of spirits beyond any imagining do not possess a more poignant or compelling answer. There are those among us who know—to the most all-encompassing degree possible—what currently exists in the vastness of the Creator's never-ending horizons of consciousness. They are eternal Beings and, as such, can ultimately manifest into any world, even unto the farthest reaches of their divine vision and knowing. Should these grand Beings continue on and journey forever, even they would never discover an ultimate end. Coming to understand that these pursuits, though intriguing, are ultimately unimportant, is what keeps us attuned to the most glorious call. We have found that our ultimate treasure, our greatest calling is to seek the ecstasy of expressing the love pouring forth from Source.

"Stay true to your course, as yours is the flight of awareness, attunement, and the deepest experience of all aspects of love. Set your sights on continuing to elevate your heart and mind upward and inward. Embrace all with complete surrender as the next part of your journey brings you closer to divine love. You will not find what you are truly seeking here. Questions on the nature of the universe only result in more questions.

Hold fast to the realizations arising from within your own heart, for these hold the infinitely more significant secrets of inestimable worth to your ascension. New awakenings will continue to surface along your way. Ready yourself for the next phase of your journey which will be unlike any you have as yet experienced.

Slowly disappearing in a flash of effervescent starlight, the last sparkles of her image dissolved into space as her parting song of praise echoes within us...

"Glory be to Source, Creator of All...."

Indeed, this is a moment so precious and rare. We must hold it close and keep it dear to our hearts. We must guard this gift with a total commitment to honor it with our highest devotion.

Now we know that as ascending children of the universe, we will always be inspired, when our essence awakens through love.

A Daughter of Love sent out in deepest compassion from the heart of The Universal Mother? What more magnificent wonders can possibly await?

DIVINE CONSCIOUSNESS

Chapter Four

SOURCE

PRELUDE
♡

After countless journeys of universal awakening, becoming excited to take the next step is not unusual. Contemplating the experience of new transformational energy is always blissful, but let us take a moment before continuing. In seeking a greater understanding, we must first realize that the quest for ultimate human consciousness and growth is not always a smooth predictable path. Our travels will not always take us upward, inward, or even onward. When considering the universe, reality and multidimensional expansion, there are endless possibilities and, of course, the unexpected. These unforeseen experiences unfolded when I first reached this very summit. We shall resume our journey on the other side.

BLACKNESS

Upon leaving the Universe of Universes, there were times when I ascended into a deep dark Blackness. This was a state of knowing that I had reached many times, yet remained unable to get past, or through. During certain moments of deep immersion, intense emotions would surface and I would feel subtle ripples or perhaps waves that seemed to touch me, but never strongly enough for me to comprehend what they were. The sheer Blackness that surrounded me was complete. Each time this happened, even though there were no actual signs, I sensed that I was encountering some type of limitation.

Perceived as a barrier to my ascension, I deeply yearned to know what was beyond this lightless curtain. Yet, no answer came, and if there was a way, it did not reveal itself. Try as I might, I could never ascend past this point.

After what seemed like an eternity, I started to feel subtle sensations. Only an impression at first, it felt as if I was nudged ever so slightly by a gentle energy while being brushed by the softest caress of flower petals. Even though there was no form and the Blackness remained, this delicate embrace became my only sign that something was possibly shifting. Through the love this thrilling experience inspired in me, I eagerly desired to know more and continued to reach even higher.

There were countless visits to the Blackness, and often the wondrous phenomena of velvety flower petals embracing me returned. I longed to see what the universe was trying to show me, and my profound passion to know became all-encompassing. Emotionally, I wanted to feel where I was and what was happening to me. I had to find a way to transform my limited perceptions, even if that included releasing what I had previously deemed my highest attainments. Deep within I understood this was the only way new visions could be revealed. I knew through this desire to reach the highest of all realities, the creative spirit within would rise and show me a new way.

The Blackness itself can only be described as the complete and total omission of any color whatsoever. It was eclipsed, in that even black didn't exist. It wasn't the void or nothingness, but simply the sheer absence of all form. Gentle, peaceful, even blissful, it was quiet and all pervasive. Having reached this familiar state so many times, I almost came to the point of believing this was as far as anyone could go, as far as anyone could reach. Yet, the curious sense of floating or being suspended was reassuring. Feeling some degree of motion was present, even though I couldn't perceive it, waves and pulsations arose from time to time, sustaining and encouraging me. Perhaps I couldn't interpret or understand what was happening, but something new was developing.

Slowly, subtle fluctuations began to take place around me, and diminutive dots of pure color became visible in the tiniest fragments imaginable. Infinitesimally tiny, they flickered in and out, almost as if pure energy was propelling them. They were ever so fine little glowing dots of pulsating light the color of lilac, only lilac, apparently coming from a place formerly unseen by my natural vision. I did not understand how I could see them. Then suddenly the lilac lights would vanish. How thrilling! At last, I felt a change was finally happening.

Appearances of these dancing particles occurred with each successive visit into this state. Because of the almost ethereal nature of what I observed, I felt completely enveloped with no true sense of self, which made it impossible to determine time and space. This most delicate glistening, somehow entwined with the touch of the soft flower petals created an atmosphere that was truly exquisite.

Seeing and feeling this emergence of color produced an otherworldly sensation. It was unlike anything I had ever experienced before. Not really seeing with my eyes, it was as if my vision was resonating instead with an ecstatic emotional presence emanating through the center of my heart. A transcendent euphoria prevailed that was far in advance of any former sense of awareness.

With each visit through the Blackness, the sparkling lilac lights became denser, more frequent, and generated emotions that grew with intensity, becoming more and more loving. Shimmering and touching me through the darkness, the colors, the lights, and the sensation of petals continued to reappear. My heart expanded past limitation to fully embrace each new experience. The pinpoints of lilac flickering in and out—accompanied by the feeling of the softest, silkiest flower petals gently falling around me—were enthralling and captivating.

At last, a breakthrough occurred. Up to that instant the lucent lights had been only fleeting specks glinting from afar, but now they began glowing even brighter in their own luminescence. Miraculously, branches began to form, appearing to grow from trees made of the same lilac light. Expanding this stunning vision into view, these shapes became scintillating expressions of their own bloom. Each leaf and branch seemed to call to me, as this new life began to reveal itself. The Blackness was giving way, fading, as I was being lifted into the soft luster of a beautiful garden. Never before had I ascended to this height of consciousness.

THE FALL

♡

Just as I was bathing in the ecstasy of this glorious experience, it happened! For some reason, still unknown, through an involuntary reaction the worst possible event occurred. My eyes opened! I was so far beyond my senses, deeply in tune with what I was *seeing,* that I had completely lost my point of connection to self.

In that instant, as my physical eyes opened, *both realities*—The Lights and The Three Dimensional - existed simultaneously. Then I had the sensation I was falling. Dropping without warning, tumbling over and over for an eternity, until finally it felt like I slammed head first into a solid wall of steel. In what was both a flash and forever, my full presence was instantaneously drawn back into my body and into the room where I was sitting. *I went into total soul shock. Emotionally crushed, I just sat there shaking and trembling, questioning.... Why did this happen? Why did my eyes open?*

I was disoriented and unbalanced for what seemed like forever. Gone were the luminescent lilacs and the threshold I was about to step across...completely gone. In desperation, I asked myself over and again: *Will I ever be able to find my way back to that beauty, to that loveliness?* Falling into a deep state of depression, my feelings of hopelessness were overwhelming and all-consuming. Retreating into dreary clouds of obscure emotions, I became a recluse and life became a total blur of disillusionment. In these moments, lost and alone, I asked myself: *Whom can I speak with? Who can possibly understand my loss?* Sadly, from deep within my soul, no answer came.

After rising into those heavenly heights, gazing upon the most radiant of lights, and experiencing such a glorious gift, I had been cast back into what appeared to be the deepest of shadows. Thoroughly dejected in every sense, I was consumed by the hopeless feeling of "Paradise Lost," never knowing if I would ever again return to that ecstatic moment of bliss. Fearing the answer, I couldn't even bring myself to try. Weeping inconsolably, I mourned and grieved the devastation as much as the death of a loved one, when all hope is lost of ever seeing their radiance again. Even now, as I look back, it is still unknown how long it was before the stinging tears dried on my face. I only remember being left with an unbearable numbness and a deep, empty ambivalence of uncertainty and doubt.

Soberly, as I pondered this chain of events, I began to comprehend what might have happened. Perhaps my conscious awareness had reached a state my physical body could no longer sustain. I considered the possibility that the sheer input of that level of cognizance was too much for any physical, three-dimensional soul to uphold. I must have been so immersed in intuition and spirit that, in some way, I felt I could maintain that degree of perception, even beyond the elevated limitations of my body. I don't know why, but this appeared to be the greatest mistake I had ever made or experienced in my lifelong pursuit of personal growth and expansion.

Emotionally it felt like lifetimes passed before my complete and sorrowful dejection finally began to subside. Yet, even though my confidence had been deeply shaken, I could not forget the ecstasy, the bliss of being in that divine magnificence. Gradually, reverently, step by tentative step, I began to consider reaching again, to those higher realms. I knew I had to at least try once more. Slowly I began to heal spiritually, and optimism began to breathe back into my life force.

Only later did I understand that what really happened was an extraordinary breakthrough. A supreme truth arose with the striking realization that my consciousness was never in my body! Indeed, this was a simultaneous lightning bolt of perception and a new awakening.

Understanding shone clearly now. My consciousness has always been an individual creation of The Great Consciousness, expressing itself within me, as me. We have always been one. Never actually in my body, I was not seeing with my physical eyes, but rather through The Eye of All Consciousness. Through the continual act of pursuing and striving for transformation, unknowingly or perhaps even naively, an expanded refinement of sight had developed. In perceiving this state of all-embracing awareness, the greatest appreciation of seeing a singular vision had risen as the highest experience of the lilac blooms. No longer looking through two eyes, my sight was complete and unified. At the very least, reaching this type of enlightenment promised that it was ultimately possible to become aware of being in Presence itself.

Encouragement began to arise within me, as I remembered the conscious act of loving and the heartfelt yearning for more were what initially inspired me. With an expanded sense of confidence, my hopes and dreams cautiously returned, and I set out to break through what were previously viewed as obstacles. My heart began to open and, ultimately, it expanded far past all former limitations, revealing an elevated awareness and bestowing me with the ability to truly see for what seemed like the first time. The desire within me continued to search through the darkness, drawing me forward. Somehow, I knew there was something wondrous awaiting me, something far grander than anything I had ever known.

It took some time to readjust my heart focus as I ascended through the multiple layers of awareness and boundless textures of consciousness. Finally, I attained the intimate state of Blackness again. But this time I understood what it was. I remained calm and blissful, as I centered myself and simply allowed the events to unfold as they were meant to. I didn't know if this would work the same way it had when I first began. My confidence grew and I became even more inspired, empowering my heart to open and pursue my search into the next realization, whatever it might be.

Then, in one of the most thrilling moments of my life, the sparkle of lilac began to appear, once more. Brighter and more dazzling they became, shining as luminescent wonder upon wonder. It was as if an impenetrable boundary had been revisited and overcome. I had reached the Blackness once again, but this time it slowly faded, withdrawing around me as I ascended into a lovely bath of the warmest lilac petals. The light shone in a way that could only be experienced through the newly expanded vision my heart had been granted. Exalted emotion rippled through me, as I was now in the midst of a glorious garden of the most beautiful lush lilac blooms. Sweeter than my sweetest memory, outshining my dearest hope and surpassing all imagination, ultimate gratitude poured from me as I basked in the glow of sublime bliss!

THE GARDEN OF LILAC

Petals were falling all around me in the softest float of lilac, adorning this loveliest of gardens and filling the air with an ambient bouquet, exquisite and rare. I found myself deep within the embrace of the lilac blooms, aglow with their own inner radiance. Deeply moved by their beauty, delighting in their delicate fragrance, an even greater appreciation for all life and creation was awakened within me. The perfection flowing from Source itself had come alive. This was Source Love, the ultimate, absolute, and supreme truth that emanates eternally throughout all Creation.

Transfixed in an all-encompassing euphoria, and with inspiration bursting from within and showered in an enthralled ecstasy, *I became one with the rapture of the Divine.*

ON THE THRESHOLD

I am sharing the events of my initial experience with the divine dimension to illustrate that even when we encounter feelings of loss, confusion, and limitation, perhaps even lamenting the devastation of our failures, there is always the promise to begin anew. This eternal nature of enlightenment will always reawaken us. Even if we fall and missteps are made, the universe is always there to show us the way forward. In truth, there are no mistakes. Every step is ultimately a lesson learned, for if we keep reaching through the supreme power of Presence, Universal Love will always reach back.

Now, finding ourselves in this inspiring Garden of Lilac through the retelling of this experience, our journey resumes.

Stretching out before us we see the space before and around us has expanded into the entire color spectrum of lilac. Vibrant, self-illuminating forests and gardens of celestial fascination are all around us. There are blossoms of purple and violet, lavender and amethyst reflecting golden hues flowering from the deep indigo roots gracing the effervescent auric tip of every lilac bloom.

THE MANDORLA

Coming into view, we see something quite rare and extraordinary. Prior to this moment, everything we have seen looked like a garden of limitless horizons stretching out into a multidimensional panorama. Now there appears a faint dome arcing above us, as simultaneously there is also a reversed dome, emerging and curving beneath us. Looking all around, in every direction, we realize we are suspended between these two points of evanescence. We have risen into the center point of a Mandorla.

A Mandorla occurs as an overlapping space where two separate dimensional spheres of reality intersect. Here, the unique Divine Spirit Realm we are entering is marked by the cradling dome beneath us that we have stepped across and entered. This Divine Dimension interacts and is superimposed over the spatial Cosmic Sphere we are leaving.

The reality of this connectivity is reminiscent of two flower petals, with a portion of one laid on and over the other. Between the sphere-shaped petal of the Cosmic Dimension and its vibrational boundaries arcing upward, is a similar shaped petal of the first hint of the Divine Dimension, growing stronger as it reaches downward to welcome us. In the space between these two overlapping dimensions there is a glowing center point. This is where the Garden of Lilac exists. This rare vision of these two worlds, these two different states of perception, is clearly visible as from the Garden of Lilac we can see both vanishing points.

The cosmic energy translation of space-time transitions upward, vibrationally overlapping with this unique interaction of the divine, and becomes the place where both realities exist simultaneously. In a fleeting moment, as time falls away, we are elevated through the highest emotional frequencies of love, reaching solely into the realm of the timeless divine.

Making our way to this point, we understand why our journey has seemed so wondrous. In essence, this overlapping is a combination of, and an interaction between, two states of consciousness is often referred to as the *Vesica Piscis*. Here lies the mystical interaction of space and non-space, location and non-location. We are viewing the seamless convergence of these realities as we transition into the celestial. Suspended in the midst of this blending of the cosmic and the divine, we witness the delicate garden of purest lilac as a vista point, a magnificent portal in the midst of this majestic Mandorla.

THE DOVE

From above, a flash of shimmering, lustrous white suddenly appears and slowly descends into the garden. Reaching a branch overhead, we behold The Dove. Glistening and iridescent, The Dove's translucent body shines with its own light.

We have arrived in the land where The Dove resides.

Universally, The Dove is seen as a heavenly messenger, love's highest expression of unity and peace. In this exalted garden, her rays perpetually emanate the grandest of all joys. Not until an individual has unified these qualities within his or her own heart and made their way here are they able to merge with the Divine. The Dove symbolizes the degree of personal as well as supreme love that must be present to rise beyond this point.

A depth of wisdom through the acquisition of knowledge might come to be known by virtue of the mind. Observing many different evolutionary schemes of life can also give rise to abundant insight. A subtle barrier exists to this approach, however, because mind can never truly know that which is not of itself. Freeing ourselves from these illusive obstacles, our hearts can expand beyond these limitations.

The brilliance represented here in the garden is a reflection of the awakened inner qualities essential to transcend all cosmic illusions and fly on, into the infinite.

The Dove floats beside us, and her message gently resonates as emotions understood from within....

"Journeying here, you have observed and experienced many of Creation's magnificent celebrations and encountered awe-inspiring vistas and mystical revelations along your way. These represent the highest and most profound events of your life. Recall every moment and how it moved you, allowing yourself to bask in each blissful awakening to the finest detail.

"Each experience is a miracle to be sure, yet to hold on to them as the most cherished memories you have ever had will only lead you to a wonderful end, nevermore to reach another. Remember and express appreciation and gratitude for each step along your journey, but do not revere them and make them your all. Instead, savor the anticipation of knowing that ahead lies an infinite realm of possibility. No matter how high you travel, no matter how memorable your experiences may be, or how exhilarated you might feel, Source is ever-present, patiently waiting to show you what exists in vistas beyond the imagination of your most transcendent dreams.

"Embrace this moment leading to the exalted states that await you now. Feel the rush emerging and the exhilaration of diving into yet another possibility. A new radiance surrounds you and, yes, an even greater expression of the divine awaits, calling out to your essence.

"Only in becoming the love that flows from your heart, can you cross the expanse from where you are into the awaiting world of ecstasy. I am here to help lift you across the divide. This is where your most exalted aspirations and desires will be transformed into their grandest expression and exquisite experience. It has always been through me, the ultimate expression of peace, serenity, and bliss-filled love, that this crossing becomes possible. Embrace the place within your heart that knows no boundaries and passes all understanding. This is where the effusion of Source animates your soul. From deep within this eternal well of love, we fly to the shores of the infinite.

"Soon, you will enter a state of knowing beyond the universe of appearance and events. This is where the qualities you have been seeking resolve into the singular vision of oneness.

"As you step into this river of flowing life, let it pour through you. Bask in its wonders as you continue onward, but hold on to nothing, because soon you will experience everything."

The Dove floats beside us, her wings outstretched. Centered in this still point, wave after wave engulf us in the tides of exalted love. Reverence and gratitude for all that has been given blends perfectly with the excitement and anticipation of these next moments.

Nestled in her downy embrace, away we fly. Higher and higher the intensity of purest energy rises. Leaving the cosmic realms completely behind, we expand through the invisible dome of the Mandorla into the purely divine. The Dove begins to beam brighter and brighter, until with one last great burst, she vanishes!

THE IMAGINAL

Finding ourselves at the zenith of our journey, we have entered into the *Imaginal*, the place where our travels speak the language of vision alone.

Ultimate awareness of the genius of our soul is essential for attunement with Imaginal realities. This requires a delicate, subtle, and total transformation. These paths are made unique by the spiritual perceptions of those who travel them. Entering the Imaginal world now, life rises up to manifest all that we seek for completion. By our invitation, the Universe will bring us experiences that mirror infinite ideas and treasures, creating a personal alchemy unavailable in our everyday world. A purer more open self is available only when realized through direct perception of the Inner Eye.

Attunement with the sacred exists in the reality of the Imaginal. A sublime sensation permeates the very atmosphere, where anything is possible, yet everything is contained. Mere words will no longer serve us here. This realm of amplified awareness will quicken the realization and revelation of our greatest personal truth.

Embracing what can only be known as *Divine Love*, the desire to travel has evaporated into a rapturous sense of arrival. Limitations do not exist in this expression of Oneness. Our experience of the constant pulsation of reality waves reaching out into infinity no longer commands our attention.

We seek to know, to define what this Imaginal place is, yet even before our thought is complete, the answer is given. The Imaginal is akin to a confluence or blending point where phenomenon falls away and each has purely become their own Eye of the Beholder.

Where every-thing and no-thing converge, where happening and no-happening overlap, we are in that indescribable state of presence where only a subtle sense of our own inner essence exists. Time and eternity do not reside here!

Surrendering totally, a new story begins.

THE FLUTE

Out of nothing and nowhere we begin to perceive a soft echo, the mirroring of a silvery glint upon our inner eye. A cloud-like mist surrounds an incomprehensible appearance of the finest and most meticulous latticework, composing something unknown. Faint, at first, it slowly starts to appear. Only the whisper of an outline becomes evident, but soon we sense that the shimmering silvery lines are interacting and identifying with each other. Displaying but the sheerest silhouette, at last we can finally envision what is being created. Coming forth now, materializing from a brilliant sterling gleam, an elegant concert flute comes into being. The shape and contour of the flute become denser and denser until it has become what appears to be a solid object with substance, created right before us. What has guided these mercurial strands to fashion this delicate flute, and why, is a mystery.

What is obvious though, is that as it reaches the fullness of its design it has been touched by the divine and given consciousness and awareness. That is to say, the flute *knows* it is a flute!

This instrument remains as yet untested, unaware of its mission or purpose, and perhaps wondering why it exists at all. Disoriented and without direction, the flute seems to be simply waiting. We feel a *wooosh* rushing past us and instinctually know that this is the very first breath that will ever flow through the flute, animating its mystical nature to create its song. Enthralled by this spectacle, we witness its keys beginning to move, as if being played by an unseen hand. Responding to the first breath pouring through it, the keys move somewhat stiffly, rigidly, even awkwardly at first. The flute does not yet know what is being asked of it, or what to play. It has, after all, never played anything before. Slowly adapting to this movement, its keys begin to synchronize and the flute begins to respond to the creative flow, producing its first simple refrains. Because it is a wonderfully perfect instrument, as perfect as any material creation can be, the flute begins trying to emulate and express that perfection. Within and through this inner desire, the life of the flute begins to unfold before our eyes.

An initial connection between the creative hand of the unseen artist, the breath flowing through the flute, and the flute itself is established from its inception. Even though all three interact in the same instant, the quality of the music we hear, see, and feel is only the most basic expression, at first. As slightly more complex impulses are felt within, an intense desire begins to emerge from the flute as it attempts to grasp what is happening. In the attunement of its essence as an instrument of creation, the flute feels the need to give the very best authentic quality of its inner nature.

Oh yes, the flute does have emotions, with love being the grandest of all. Through the act of expressing the creative unseen artist, the breath of life flowing through it, and the nature of its own existence, its intrinsic qualities are continuously embellished. The flute can feel, intuit, and express the total range of emotional joys and sorrows as the flow of creativity pours through it.

Coming to life, the nature of this ingenious and gifted instrument is being transformed into oneness with Divine Consciousness. The flute gives its all to the creative breath that gives it life and does its best to grow and become accomplished. Due to its very nature, however, the evolutionary journey toward its ultimate refinement is one of ebb and flow.

At first, the flute cannot interpret the impulse of the creativity flowing through it. The result is dissonance and a lack of clarity in the musical themes performed. Through these feelings of discord, misconceptions occur as it continually tries to self-correct and adjust. When unsuccessful, the saddest of songs weep softly through its keys. These are moments of limitation and anguish, as the flute's desire to explore its abilities and expand its talents burns intensely. The saddened and sorrowful sound of its unfulfilled yearning spill out as the tears of captivating rhapsodies and melodies in songs and refrains of deep lament. These are some of its most poignantly haunting compositions, reflecting profound disappointment, grief, and regret. The flute experiences the entire range of feelings imbued with the complexity and texture of all emotions, including the ultimate anxiety when out of balance with the expression of its divine life.

The unseen artist is aware of these initial frailties and imminent limitations. Steadily, with gentle hand and loving heart, the artist guides the music through the keys into existence and through its song, creates the life of the flute. As the artist's loving energy continually pours forth, the flute is slowly able to respond. Constantly evolving, longing to be free from impending limitations, it strives to express, through the quality of each note played, what is perceived to be its very best. Soon, the flute begins to explore more complex musicality, wide-ranging harmonies, and multiple themes ringing out in synchronous expression.

Comprehending the creative visionary hand upon it with better fluidity, the flute is able to respond more intuitively and with greater sensitivity, co-creating each new level flowing through it with ingenious inspiration. What was once a repeating refrain of saddened, tear-laden laments gives way to marvelous soaring melodies reaching toward the mystical source of its creation. One of the flute's inherent qualities is the deepest desire to reach for and express that which it distinguishes as its unique identity.

The spaces between the notes become the silent testimony of the flute's life, as it continues to unfold into existence. This is how it learns to contemplate the ongoing complexities of coordinating mind and emotion, and integrating this perception into its next performance. Pausing, through introspection, the flute gains insight into what has previously transpired and can interpret and consider how it has grown and what must still be accomplished. Possessing the ability to envision itself, the flute evolves and a point of integration is achieved. Advancing through this development of self-awareness empowers the flute, bestowing further refinement and enhancing the beauty of its ultimate song. Blending together its understanding, intuition, and expression, new tools of facility are fashioned and newly illuminated.

Reflecting upon the struggles and joys, the sorrows and celebrations of life, the flute has come to understand that by willfully surrendering itself into alignment and balance, its song is able to reach its highest and purest perfection. The fashioning of these transformational forces into a unified expression becomes paramount in actualizing this vision of attainment. At this moment, an epiphany arises. *A breakthrough is at hand.*

This was no easy challenge for the flute to overcome. Simply wanting to be better did not unlock the door to realizing its desires. Striving *to be* better through dedication and mastery of its gifts did. Mixing its freed yearnings with the focused expression of song gave birth to the most profound musical moments of its life. Having gained expansive vision, the flute sees that through alignment and unification with the creative artist's hand, the breath of life and its own highest qualities, it has been fused into one identity. It has fashioned a soaring vehicle to realize its greatest desires.

The flute has come alive, bursting free from its former limitations. We can hear and feel its unique individuality spilling out in an ecstasy of song, expressing the longing of its deepest love. Striving to navigate the various phases from its origin through ongoing evolution, and reaching ever higher to unite with its true calling, inspires us to mirror the nature of this achievement. In doing so, we see and feel both its sadness and joy. The frustration and exhilaration of striving toward and finally accomplishing the breakthrough into freedom is the personification of bliss itself. Continuing to grow, creating monumental artistry with the divine, the flute has mastered the many melodies that were once far beyond its capabilities.

Witnessing this continued growth and inner process of perfection and awareness, we notice the flute has slowly begun to transmute into a subtle shift of colors. It has transformed from the shiny bright silver image when it was first created, into the most beautiful of golden hues. Its body, brilliantly polished and lustrous, empowers its ability to rise even further above its previous imperfections. The awareness and consciousness of the flute merge with the emotions of its deepest desire. We witness divine emergence joining the embodiment of richness and fullness this instrument was created to be, as *the flute becomes the music itself.*

Many challenges were encountered along the way when obstacles threatened to halt the progress of the flute's development. Often, it was faced with the ultimate decision of choosing to remain forever in a dissonant state, or overcoming difficulties and hindrances. The flute chose to embrace the challenges and, thus, attained the golden era of its life. Its music is as near to perfection as any can be, united in oneness with the supreme origin of its creation.

The golden flute gleams in its transformation and is a wonder to behold. Having reached the zenith of its abilities, the soaring notes flow out to the height and depth of their conception. The towering melodies and magnificently inspired harmonies lift us out of our own limitations to touch and be touched in the very core of our inner soul light. The expression of the flute's mastery with the unseen hand upon it has ushered in a glorious golden age of transformational evolution. Now it brings to light the universal lyrical inflections of the deepest of experiences that all life embraces, the music that lives within us all.

Grand performances of the vast spectrum of vision and emotion, love and desire, emanate freely and effortlessly from the animating brilliance of its soul. The keys seem to move as one, by its near perfect Will and the artist's hand upon it. Gone are the laments of sadness and melancholy. Out of the calmness of ultimate confidence rises excitement and a consummate gratitude for this triumphant moment of spiritual fulfillment!

The flute continues resonating ever purer tones unto its crowning culmination, but now once again, profound changes are being reflected. Slowly, we see the release of its golden glow, as it inexplicably begins to transform into the finest of hardwoods. Continuing its evolving nature, this new expression produces an entirely different kind of sound.

Having been through the initial stages of development, the flute has found its talent for genius. Mature and farseeing, it has reached its completeness of its highest potential. Viewing the maturity through the transformational evolution that the flute has become, we find its music is both transcendent and profoundly moving. The fluid integration of artist, breath, and melody, now a divine unity, is the most inspiring of visions.

The glorious musical streams, cascading into the most beatific of colors, rise and flow on, reaching toward Source. Beginning its expression through the flute, the music has become something of its own. It has surpassed the limitations of the very instrument it took its shape, form, and life from. Brilliantly, the music pouring from the flute soars beyond all former confinements.

In reaching for its highest expression, the flute ultimately realizes itself as spirit. Through the continually broadening ascending motifs moving in an upward spiral, the flute flowers into the totality of its song, releasing itself from the corresponding forces of material dissolution.

As the deeply polished hardwood of the flute gradually starts to chip away and disintegrate, its keys, still attempting to play effortlessly, are not responding very well. It cannot reproduce its former mastery. Circles of the original silvery light appear at each end of its body, and in deliberate fashion they slowly begin spiraling toward each other until they meet at the center to complete this process. The flute, once again, is completely transformed.

The hardwood body, which has fallen away piece by piece, cannot maintain its integrity of creation. As it begins to surrender to its own resolution, a nostalgic, exquisite counterpoint of ascending and descending refrains ring out.

Sacred beyond all measure, the descending melodies resound in a wonderful expression of purest gratitude as the finest wood falls slowly and completely away, leaving only the original tremulous outline of its first lightness of being. This outline vibrates for a breathless moment in silent reverence, in pure fulfillment, and then its shining shimmer begins to diminish. The silvery latticework is becoming detached. In a subtle flash the image of the flute completely disappears and this sacred vision can only be said to be a treasure of remembrance and appreciation, richness and admiration.

But the music. Oh, the music! It *continues on* in an ascending theme, imbued with all of the experiences and memories, all of the emotions and evolution, every glory-filled experience the flute was created to realize. The insights and divine visionary expressions uniquely and perpetually created through its existence take on a new and unique individual shape and character, as the richness of what was once the life of the flute wholly frees itself from its material limitations. Having achieved its own unity and identity, the song of the flute advances forever upward, inward, and onward to begin an unknown and unique journey, seeking Source.

The flute gave everything it had to become its most accomplished self, masterfully succeeding in doing so by becoming one with the unseen artist's hand. Finding the way to expand and redefine itself by allowing the breath of life to emanate through it without restraint, it freely expressed every particle of its essence to become that breath. The flute knew its consciousness. The flute united in Oneness. The flute became its own transcendence. Now, homeward bound as a ravishing one-of-a-kind unity, its eternal essence remains replete with all the music ever played from first inception to new beginning.

Only the best and purest qualities of its former lifetime go through this process of refinement. Only the truest, purest essence of all the life that was lived is drawn out and into this accompanying transition.

The energy streams are the grandest realizations of what once was, but has now risen to unconditional attainment. Coalescing into a gleaming collection of the most evolved qualities, gleaned through the flute-life's every encounter with the challenges of its evolution, the limited personality of what was once the flute has been released to the past, embracing this moment of glorious Presence.

Expanding into an invisible center-point, out of which all future potential will redesign and emanate its developed qualities, there is a new and original existence coalescing.

The energy currents of vibrational coherence have rewoven themselves and been reborn into their own unique identity. No longer seeing itself as an object, a far-reaching perception of a completed identity is streaming from this inner effusive energy center of rebirth. The swirls from within it burn brighter and brighter, interacting and fashioning a different vehicle, another original expression of creation. In the beginning was the flute, and that life was lived to the fullest, but that actuality is no more. There is only a greater brilliant Being stepping into its next vision of evolution. This advanced, glorious, and brilliant Being turns its face to a newly discovered destiny of sentience and awakening.

The Unseen Master's Hand now fully appears and becomes fused as the perpetual guiding light along the eternal path of this newly emerged, original creation, reborn to strive once again into the glory of Divine Oneness.

Here is where the miracle occurs. The essence of what was contained in the Being once known as *The Flute*, now without reservation, feels the love of its creator. In reaching this new rebirth of soul identity, it realizes its immeasurable worth and knows it is loved completely by the Divinity that brought it into this Imaginal life. For so long it had sought this love, trying to be good enough, hoping to realize itself, and always wanting more. As it rematerializes into a new life, a new journey, it feels and knows fully that it has always been good enough.

Being received in acceptance and tenderness, the sons and daughters of this new land reach out to embrace and welcome home their precious child. In a celebration of glorious awakening, this extraordinary expression of the Divine birth is given a *new name* and will forever be known as, Tysargus!

OUR OWN LIVES

It is easy to see why we have come to the Imaginal and how this creation and the ultimate transformation of the flute so closely resemble our own lives. Are we not instruments ourselves, striving to express the very breath of life flowing through us? Is it not our destiny to experience and know the divinity from which we came? What the silvery streams have shown us—through the enfoldment of the flute's evolution and its ultimate ascension beyond its body into a new birth—is the deepest contemplation and aspirations of our own spiritual journey.

Taking a step back and viewing the grandeur of this process, and feeling the breath of life flowing through us, we can experience the melodies of our personal life playing through our own heart song. Divine unity can uplift and enhance our life to rise past dissonance, frustration, and sadness into the harmony and joy of our heart's desire.

The beauty and splendor of the sounds flowing forth from the flute resonate the songs of our own sorrows and happiness. The tears and laughter of our lives are mirrored in each of our personal remembrances and experiences. Releasing our most difficult misfortunes, while embracing our most promising moments of inspiration, brings greater appreciation of the wisdom and strength we have gained and the beauty that remains throughout this journey of life.

To hear The Master's Song, to feel The Breath of Life through the act of loving and being loved, is the ultimate pinnacle of any life. The true inner mystery we must all ultimately face is revealed. *Will our song, enriched and enlightened, rise in liberation, playing on even as our own personal instrument falls away?*

Standing in the Imaginal, awakening to this glorious vision, there is but a singular thought remaining....

What will my song be?

We are creations of Source, yet we rarely hear its guidance through mere words. Divinity has utilized myth amid the backdrop of the Imaginal. Opening our soul through the experience of love and personal empathy, we are eternally woven through the conscious presence of our own reality. This is where each one can drink in their innermost thoughts and feelings, and appreciate the quality of life they are creating. Here we encounter a knowing that reaches past mere mind and into the very core of creation.

Each of us, in any single moment of observance along this journey of the flute, can suddenly exclaim, "There. That is me. That has happened to me. Those sad longings and exquisite joys have all been part of my experience, my life's song. I know what that feels like. Now I can see what was being shown to me." Only through inner essence, which is our song, can we come to know and infuse these profound revelations as our life plays on.

It wasn't that the flute didn't encounter obstacles and frustration. The moments of challenge were many and often. The flute just never felt fulfilled living a life of dissonance, and it refused to be trapped in a melody that did not express its authentic self. Instead, through the dauntless courage of its own will and faith, and believing that it could be more, the flute played on through the challenges.

We too, most assuredly will encounter our own obstacles along the way. Knowing our song is a reflection of the life we create; we can choose to embrace harmony and live in blessings and love. Regardless of the life conditions that might prevail, the way to create our own heart's desire is always there.

We are not destined to remain trapped in an unending chorus doomed to playing a dissonance of our own design. Through our greatest abilities we can create happiness, living life to the fullest. Like the flute, we can choose to see the reality we live as the music of life.

As we follow our own path, we are often confronted by life's ultimate questions. Often the answers seem simple and the way ahead assured. But, all too soon the way disappears and we find ourselves lost once again. In becoming our own inner light, we realize we have always been on the path and the horizon of our true significance and authenticity shines through these perceptions. We can come to ask the most important and significant questions, and most especially, hear the truth from within our heart echoing back to us from Source.

Who am I? You are a unique and divine instrument of creation, crafted by the unseen artist, designed and gifted to respond to the Breath of Life flowing through you. Your ingenious, inspirational nature exceeds your known and unknown limitations, expanding beyond the possible and impossible into a universe awaiting your discovery.

Why am I here? You are here to master this instrument by discovering the truth of love you are, and shine that brilliant love into the evolutionary quality of your life. As you encounter and overcome the agonies and ecstasies of Life, you will ultimately discover you are crafting your innermost soul and becoming the effortless expression of essence and love. This is the rapture that you have always sought to awaken in your heart of hearts.

What is my purpose? Your purpose is to discover and embrace the light that gives life through the inherent faith present in the gift of your indomitable Will. When tempered with focus, your Will can dissolve the distractions of false beliefs that stand between you and the truth of your pure presence. These qualities are there, lying dormant within you. Once embraced and forged through life's experience, these intrinsic virtues become the steadfast beacons guiding your way. By casting off doubt and limitation, through strength of

Will, nothing can separate you from living your most magnificent and extraordinary life.

Contemplating our inner reality cannot merely be reflections of words. A divine identity has been bestowed upon us. We must come to know this identity as our own personal truth. The authenticity of this truth, unique unto every life, resonates as the song of each voice crying out to know.

As awareness flowers into self-realization, we become the music, the pure radiant song of our own life. In feeling the Unity of All, peace beyond understanding is born within. The questions we asked when we first embarked on this journey were profound. The answers, shining like jewels, are the treasures that lay revealed before us.

Although we might wish to remain here, basking forever in the wondrous experience of the Imaginal, ultimately the moment to return will soon be upon us. Knowing we can, if we wish, bring these qualities of enlightenment into the lives we continue to live is both rapturous and sublime.

The purpose of this journey has always been to harmonize the growing realization of love's attainment fused with the expansion of our consciousness. With the treasures of insight we have received along the way, culminating here in The Imaginal, the qualities of our evolving soul can be uplifted beyond measure. The life we are living *now* can take on greater purpose and higher meaning.

Allow the divine experience of The Flute Life and the glorious energy streams reshaping themselves into a brilliant new birth, to surround you with the feelings of warmth, hope and the purest light of love.

As that resonance still echoes in our hearts, the slightest sense of motion returns as the Imaginal begins to dissolve. A loving affection permeates the reappearing space around us, and we become aware of an intimate familiar presence.

THE RETURN

The Dove appears, and once again we feel the perfect peace and serenity of her soft downy embrace.

Tenderly folding her wings around us, she is even more beautiful than before. Everything is more beautiful. Even our former understanding of beauty itself pales in comparison to the vast reaches and majesty of this creation of eternity.

In parting, the message of The Dove softly resonates within us....

"As your consciousness continues its spiritual attunement, the yearning to return will forever rise within you. Your heart will always remember this sacred path to the Divine. When you seek me through the deepest expression of your soul's desire, I will be there, and our journey to the highest visions of divine ecstasy will begin anew."

Soaring through the everlasting expanse of eternity, we fly on until we are, once more, suspended between the two dimensions of the Mandorla. Ever so gently, The Dove unfolds her wings releasing us to float freely, surrounded by the luminescent garden of lilac. The Dove slowly fades from our sight and withdraws in one last burst of evanescence.

Our emanations become slightly more opaque, until

we see the cosmic sparkling splendor of the extraordinary realm of universes.

Being drawn along the exquisite energy spiral, the connected strands of living light encircle our images, resplendent in their sheen. Blissful and entranced, we gaze into the vast choirs with endless inspiration streaming forth on glistening beams. The play of creative flow is eternally intermingling within the ever-changing dance of life. These sights, these sounds, this marvelous moment of exaltation, will be emblazoned upon our memories forever.

In the silent awe of inspiration, we are one with the magic of this moment. New dimensions await discovery as we pursue the unified desire to grow into our totality. Seeking first to know the deepest love from Source, our heart and inner wisdom expand infinitely. Eternally imprinted into our very core, radiant love beyond description shines on. Effortlessly we flow, revisiting our previously traveled wonders, until all that remains is the immense backdrop of dark energy by which the cosmic splendor of all Creation is visible.

Raying out once again from the heart of The Universal Mother, we feel the welcoming wonder of the gleaming Daughter of Love. Infusing us with glowing effervescence, her warmth and support envelops us completely. Our journey has taken us far beyond the heights of our first encounter, yet still, The Daughter of Love remains one of our most breathtaking experiences. The magnificence of her spirit sings through the heart of our souls as her final message is bestowed....

"Unknown to you, many of us have witnessed your inspiring journey. We are pleased to see that you have remained steadfast to your divine truth.

"There has been much joy in watching you embrace the path to the highest pinnacle of your desire. It is a beauty to behold seekers along the eternal way making courageous choices that lead to experiences of unparalleled union with Source.

"The light that shines in and around you will forever and eternally be present in the heart of the Universal Mother. Draw strength from the knowledge that we are always here. Should the call ever go out, our cosmic paths will meet once again. We are forever waiting with pure devotion, ready to assist all seekers. May the perpetual presence of love always shine forth, illuminating your way."

Slowly, within our vision of her gleaming spirit, the Daughter gently begins to soften. The sparkling starlight from whence her glow originated disappears into radiance, delicately diffusing into a vision, glorious beyond imagining.

Soon only endless space remains, floating in the brilliance amidst the countless miracles of the cosmos we can feel our emanations delicately re-tuning our heart waves.

Again, we experience the thrill of the eternal Beings championing all creations unfolding within the Universe of Universes. Glowing within their radiance is the myriad of mystical luminosities within each local star cluster and the countless trillions of life expressions within their charge. Sent as the Sons and Daughters of Divine Source, they mirror and reflect the gift of life to the farthest reaches of eternity.

The line that separates us from our realm, shimmering and gleaming, stands ready to receive us back. There before us, the magnificent fountain of liquid light, symbol of The Great Being who empowers our space, pours forth its eternal flow of life-giving essence.

Once more the exalted ones bid us farewell, as we are drawn into our universe. Countless space creations, shown in superb detail, radiate out from the darkness to call us home.

Quasars are burning brightly. Fiery nebulae are striving to give birth in an endless flash of the cosmic symphony. These are star-arrayed Beings for which the concept of eternity ultimately has no meaning.

Look! There in the distance the Mighty Angel from our home universe appears, the gleaming orb of light shining from his outstretched hand as if to welcome us. Projecting from the center, his brilliant image is clearly visible, suspended within the rays of the multicolored torus field. Our flowing love moves us to meet him. His message vibrates within, to the depths of our heart....

"Grow strong in the power of soul you now are. Let it pour from you, perpetually giving forth so that all can become One with Source, from which eternal illumination emanates.

"Give freely, for as you give, more will be given unto you, and that which you are will be enriched beyond the fullness of your dreams. This gift belongs to all, and all shall be granted this knowing when they wish it from the heart. Your essence is elevated through life and living, lifting you to the highest. Through the acts of your evolving soul, you become aware of all, refining your oneness with Source.

"Bring the truth of love unrestrainedly. That which you receive from Source is inexhaustible. Through these acts, you will soar in divine unity forever."

The Mighty Angel, his message complete, is once again ablaze, replete in rainbows of color as he withdraws into the rippling torus field of his first appearance. As the portal closes, magnificent arcs of dazzling swirls envelop him completely and his essence dissolves back into starlight.

As his powerful words resonate around and within us, the transcendent visions so recently witnessed, pass before our eyes. This has been a journey like no other. It has revealed to us that a soul can only traverse the unseen dimensions of life through the expansion of heart and mind. Humanity's place within the greatest of cosmic dramas is shining.

In truth, the sheer scope and grandeur of what we have envisioned is less than a speck of our own self-created shadows. It is a mere particle of the miraculous Creation shared by all life.

Our surroundings are becoming a bit clearer. The

colors around us are slightly less dazzling, although still brilliant in their splendor.

Continuing on to our local system of stars and galaxies, beckoning to us, at last we see the Milky Way. Passing through its lightless center, we witness the familiar spiral swirl of its billions of stars. Our sun, known in ancient times as the mythical Apollo, beams brightly, radiating the life-giving vitality that nourishes our green planet with its lovely cloak of blue.

UNITY CONSCIOUSNESS

Chapter Five

UNITY

TRASARA REVISITED

Before our final return, we stop to revisit the captivating floating city of Trasara and its Beings of Light.

Our guide from our previous visit, seeming to know where we have journeyed, rejoins us. Pausing in reverence and wonder, we take in the captivating panorama of the city, marveling at its atmosphere of wisdom, beauty, and love.

It would be so tempting to remain here, basking forever in the glorious rays of Trasara.

"How did your people come to create this place? Has it always been so spectacular?" we ask our guide.

Hearing our question, he becomes more serious and begins recounting the evolutionary story of the wondrous city....

THE TALE

Looking back into our hazy unknown origins, the days were very different then. Our inner life force was confined to much denser bodies. Everyone and everything appeared to be separate. Just emerging from the renaissance of self-awareness, our state of Universal Consciousness had not yet reached its fullness.

Still lingering from the early days of our evolutionary struggles, a brutish element was present within many whose progress had not kept pace. Depending on the degree to which these primitive impulses had been mastered, these factions caused havoc and confusion, often inflicting pain upon those around them.

Traveling far beyond our origins and unfortunately not having yet achieved the full transition of completion, the people had lost touch with that primal divine spark within.

We had evolved to the state where "we knew that we knew," but we still had not reached the awareness of our true nature.

In those days, the ideals of unity as a people were scoffed at by many and treasured by very few. The vast majority of our inhabitants were focused only on competition for material possessions and wealth.

Personal acquisition had become all-important, and most individuals chose to gather unto themselves every material possession they could, forsaking all others except perhaps those few they cherished.

THE OLD RULING ORDER

In the midst of this low point of spiritual growth and moral stagnation, there were opportunists who took advantage of these circumstances by seizing control and attempting to rule by force.

Whole cultures were divided and came to be labeled according to their ethnic origins. Imaginary borders were drawn and redrawn *ad infinitum* on the surface of our planet, with the opportunists staking claim of ownership to particular regions, which became home to those cultures. Coming to believe, over time, that certain countries and lands belonged to them, many of these ethnicities became nationalized, claiming certain lands to be theirs and theirs alone. This divided us even further. Many of these regions were constantly at odds, through the misconception of the differences and blood feuds, which they perpetuated aggressively. Wars raged on continually and there was ongoing deprivation, death, and destruction between clashing armies to prove who was right, and who was wrong. "This is OUR land," was the cry and credo of each warring nation. The old order did everything possible to maintain these divisions, keeping the people from uniting in the spirit of cooperation. Subtle or forced indoctrinations were manipulated for millennia, as false nationalities were formed and supported. These misplaced loyalties became totally ingrained into the fiber of life, appealing to our early transformative experiences in which a deep-rooted tribal mentality of exclusivity had prevailed.

Operating behind the scenes, like puppet masters in the dark, the old order sought to control everyone and everything, fostering conflict and separation, while making huge material gains and profits from the struggles. Whole regions of our planet were pitted against each other, secretly keeping the people in ignorance and blinding them to peaceful means of partnership and collaboration.

Advancing an insidious, elitist societal programming, the old guard generated distorted beliefs. They continually bombarded the multitudes with false imperatives claiming the superiority of some, and the inferiority of others. Whole societies were indoctrinated into accepting these lies and, as time passed, these delusional beliefs became the normalized and accepted way of living. Manufacturing global catastrophes, upheaval and constant unrest, spreading overwhelming waves of terror and fear, the old elite instilled this false sense of struggle and conflict as morally justified. Promoted and embedded into the minds of generation after generation through institutions of learning, the media, communication streams, and worldwide social organizations, a flawed and misguided entitlement was established. Through all forms of deceptive propaganda, many were deceived into believing in a mentality in which the accumulation of possessions was the highest goal. The pursuit of wealth was deemed superior, admirable, and virtuous. Toiling and struggling, everyone competed to achieve a measure of credible security. Even when these goals were apparently achieved, this lifestyle was tenuous at best, because any reality that existed in the form of possessions could be washed away and lost in an instant. There was much torment and despair among us.

All forms of communication were under the control of the old guard. Artists and musicians, empaths and philosophers, humanitarians, scientists and intellectuals were all forced to conform and compromise the authenticity of their work and true inner vision. They were allowed to continue only by demonstrating responsive actions sympathetic to the aims of their oppressors. If anyone refused, it was made impossible for them to advance their work. Some even disappeared, never to be seen or heard from again. What the people were permitted to experience was subtly or blatantly controlled and censored, with the ultimate deciding power being placed in the hands of those whose only interest lay in how much wealth could be squeezed from the ignorant masses.

Completely turning their backs on us, some of the artists and scientists, inventors and philosophers knowingly presented a skewed version of their true calling and became minions and lackeys of the old ruling order. Engineering the very technology to help facilitate this planetary tragedy, they defected from their original life mission and secretly became part of the old guard, while outwardly masquerading as uncompromising bringers of knowledge. The self-proclaimed experts of their day maintained a rigid, brutal dogma and refused to acknowledge the new truths that were quietly emerging. Our people were conditioned and fed artistic and intellectual pabulum to ensure minimum advancement and diminished perceptions. Like blind sheep, we were led into spiritual, emotional, and mental confinement.

The inadequate treatment of the sick and those in need of healing was one of the most devastating elements of our life-altering dominance. New methods of wellbeing and breakthrough cures for all manner of disease were continuingly being discovered, but these findings were subverted, hidden, or suppressed in our world. After all, cures were not nearly as profitable as ongoing maintenance. It was far more lucrative to require that those requiring medical treatment pay ongoing fees to merely manage their illnesses, instead of offering definitive cures. While potential methods to wipe out all disease and illness already existed, they were secretly withheld. Keeping us in ignorance and disbelief, we forgot that robust health is our natural state. Illness and disease were subtly perpetuated, allowing this false illusion to become our pseudo-reality.

To make matters worse, the keepers of knowledge

who belonged to the mystic societies lost sight of the essential preeminent techniques of transformation. Only these special souls knew the sacred ceremonies and divine practices of spiritual awakening that had been entrusted to them long before our journey began.

Containing universal revelations and the luminous truths of our sacred creation, they were to have quickened and accelerated our growth through which initiation into the mysteries of life would flower.

Sadly, these divine blessings were also denied us.

Over time, most of the knowledge keepers within these orders, having failed in continuing the high degree of discipline, dedication, and devotion needed, could no longer sustain higher levels of consciousness. Ultimately, they lost this precious wisdom, along with their innate connection to the deepest truth of our origins.

Generation after generation of those to whom a portion of truth had been given, devolved into separate congregations of traditional ritualistic ways of living. Each claimed to be the keepers of the one and only truth, but in actuality they imparted none. True knowledge of the mystical realities of life had long since slipped beyond their grasp.

Instead, they endeavored to frighten us by advancing the doctrine of a dark force, an all-powerful evil one, who would do us harm if we failed to live according to their rules. Many generations were terrified into submission and forced to work and surrender material support, weaving these blatant treacheries into the very fabric of life. The vast majority of the population was left lost and confused, and feeling cut off with nowhere to turn.

The old ruling order saw to it that true beauty was distorted and suppressed, and any ideals that ran contrary to their strategies of total dominance were condemned and ridiculed. Whenever this approach didn't work, outright force was used to silence those who stood up for justice, and they drove out those who refused to yield. Not even the faintest glimpse of an authentic perception of truth remained. Designated as forbidden, the knowledge and wisdom of the truly advanced Beings among us lay hidden and denigrated.

When you take beauty and wisdom away from a people, all that remains is misery and despair. Sinking deeper into the darkness of the times, our strength and vitality devolved into an unrecognizable state of total apathy, ambivalence, and paralysis. *Where was there to go? What could be done?* From even the faintest echoes of this seemingly bottomless pit, no answer came.

RENAISSANCE

It has been said that nothing can stop an idea whose time has come. The universal creative energy moves relentlessly on, and those who resist are ultimately consumed by it.

In any age, there are those who pierce the veil of the unknown, reaching toward the grand horizon of the awaiting renaissance. Diverse and advanced, these exceptional men and women became the vehicles of inspired expression, the seers of an emerging, universal, creative energy flow.

New truths began to arise among the poets and philosophers, mystics and artists, scientists and visionaries, who had already moved beyond. Through them, the mysteries of our true starry birthright were envisioned, and this beauty slowly trickled out to the masses.

From the depths of deepest despair, a gentle awakening began from within. From a deeply implanted sense of love and compassion, from many different lifestyles, renewed awareness mysteriously arose and began to resonate in the hearts of a very precious few. Unknown to them at the time, they would be the essential key to the Great Awakening that would soon manifest.

THE VANGUARD

Suddenly and seemingly out of nowhere, from every medium a vanguard of creative free thinkers from every culture began to emerge.

No recognized representative or leader united them, but rather they were connected through the collective consciousness of creation. Strengthened by their enlightened sensitivity to universal energy flow, this cosmic force sought to usher in the new age.

Small but dedicated groups joined as one, with singular purpose in their hearts. They sought to put forth the standards of a mutually inclusive prosperity that each achieved, working for the benefit of all. They vowed to manifest this vision of love and bring forth the designs for a more harmonious way of living.

Often in small groups, their works were imparted directly to the inhabitants of a given region, conveying and displaying the knowledge of the deepest mysteries of life.

Slowly, but steadily, inspiration began to flourish. Poets expressed the powerful emotions that welled up from deep within this newfound liberty. Philosophers reflected on the profound undeniable truths of existence. Mystics sought to reveal the transcendent enlightenment of the highest communion. Composers created soaring music that touched all from an inner place beyond thought.

The message started to travel far and wide. Expressing this vision in countless works of art and drama, science and devotion, philosophy and empathy, singing out through each dance and every song of the soul, spreading inspiration along the way... the awakening had begun. On their canvases, artists revealed future conceptions reflecting new social dynamics. Scholars enumerated hidden doctrines, laying bare what had been the concealed truths of our unity as a people. All works were created to inspire and encourage thoughtful contemplation and collectively uplift us from the mire of indolence and apathy to a new and soaring embrace of life.

Having dominated our society for so many generations, at last an advanced science was discovered that rendered the survival of the fittest scheme obsolete.

Scientists who were also philosophers advanced a new physics that proved the existential power of spirituality and demonstrated that everything is interrelated and connected, and originating from the same Source.

Additionally, defying all explanation, in what can only be described as extraordinary and astounding, deep healings miraculously manifested in those who were previously thought to be terminally ill. Neutralizing all manner of disease, these transformations began emerging from cultures across our world. Although the masses scoffed at these events at first, they were part of the as yet undetected convergence that was being born.

Escaping the attention of the old guard, somehow these revolutionary ideas and unexplained happenings were not viewed as a threat or taken seriously.

Utilizing somewhat obscure and hidden media sources, this courageous vanguard began the task of revealing their works. Inwardly, the wisdom of their collective heart connections spoke softly to them of establishing this new freedom of expression. Even though it possibly meant risking harm to themselves and their loved ones, the desire to continue on and break through all barriers was stronger than any fear.

Their lives had to be elevated as a whole in order to resonate with the new energy about to be released. These heralds of the new dawn became united in a collective feeling, a compelling emergent emotion that whispered: *The time to act is now.*

Ours was a planet of many separate beings, sprawled out over what were, at the time, vast distances. Only in looking back can we see from our current evolutionary vantage point that these individuals were responding to the mysterious force of emergence.

Prevailing circumstances of global deprivation, indifference, and moral desolation were at the core of what inspired them to break through to a new way. Starting out in isolation, working from their own towns, cities, and nations, they grew in size through reputation and the quality of their contributions and commitment.

Only later, as the movements became known to each other, did connections form, ultimately becoming a network.

Slowly, oh so slowly, the mass consciousness began to rise. There were those who were touched and revived by the new ideas. Beginning to awaken from their long slumber, soon our people were able to comprehend the great deception that had been cast upon them.

The numbers of those in whom compassion had been reborn began to multiply. By looking favorably on the ideals of these promising new movements, innovations were developed in communications and media. Soon the inspired works of those in this newly formed soul-fusion were flowing out to reach many of the people.

Out of this elevated strength and compassion arose brilliant luminaries who advanced the standards of true equality for all peoples and the authentic wealth of universal realization. Ideals were put forth that epitomized the banners of beauty, wisdom, and love through oneness and cooperation for the collective benefit of all.

Our world was so vast, with literally billions of inhabitants. These works went out much like notes in a bottle over an ocean of airwaves, hoping that someone would find and feel their truth. At the time it seemed as though these were desperate acts, and indeed, at first they were.

Yet remarkably, through these seemingly impossible attempts to reach out and connect, a synchronous change began!

Without our knowledge, in the midst of our darkest hour, the greatest chapter of our history was about to unfold, because out of the sinking depths and descent of our cumulative amnesia, a great shift had begun. A quality that had lain dormant within our collective soul flickered on and we began to rise in our new dawning!

THE LAW OF EMERGENCE

In the original seed of every living thing there is an entire blueprint or pattern of the complete and total plan of its birth into what it was originally designed to be. Right before our eyes, in generation after generation, we observed what appeared to be this simplistic technique of nature expressing itself perpetually. This is the process through which everything that lives comes to be. As an example, even the tallest and mightiest of trees began its life as the tiniest of seeds. In this single seed lay the entire blueprint by which the majestic tree would grow, develop, and mature, destined to become the glorious fulfillment of its grand design. In looking back, we realized that the same process of becoming was designed within the unified soul of our species. The sacred conception of our designated transcendence was about to embrace a new paradigm of perfection.

A great revelation was at hand, and we recognized this evolutionary cycle was the law of emergence in action.

At last, we remembered our pure essence and how it is imbued with the natural ability to fulfill its higher purpose. Holding fast to this knowledge, we finally learned that when conditions are right the creation, whatever it might be, emerges organically to become its highest most authentic expression of self.

Our mutual insight expanded when we discovered the existence of many groups who were already developing new transformations within the cultures of their own regions. In their own quiet way, by producing unique expressions and creating a new reality, they were a living testament to the true dawn of a new life for the betterment of each and every soul! Even though only a minute fraction of the billions of beings inhabiting our planet attained this awareness and took action… they were there.

Hundreds, even thousands of organizations, with the unified intention of bringing peace to all peoples began to form. Reaching out to one another through the emerging force of this universal Law of Emergence, a planetary movement was born. From deep within the dry desert of hopelessness and against all odds, seeds planted eons ago began to sprout and take root as the expansion of love surfaced and began to flourish! In the same way a forest naturally grows, we were growing, blossoming as individual souls and bearing fruit as a collective emergent force of life!

BARRIERS

Once we reached this stage of international impact, we encountered what appeared to be an insurmountable barrier. We were shocked to realize that the totality of our race, spread over the entire face of our planet, spoke over 9,000 different languages! Acknowledging this incredibly staggering truth, we realized that in order to unify globally it was imperative to find a way to build a bridge of true communication and overcome this greatest of obstacles.

As movements began connecting across our planet, our inability to communicate became apparent. Finding the key to translate and fully express the new profound truth across the multicultural and multilingual complexities and beyond the scores of different mindsets would be daunting. Language itself would have to be transformed.

As our history developed, life had become so mental in its orientation that we relied, for the most part, on language as our sole means of exchanging information. We soon realized the very thought, or the act of thinking, had been causing our problems all along. It wasn't that thinking is bad, quite the contrary. The ability to think is one of our most powerful natural senses. However, it was also the device the old ruling order had manipulated to advance its agenda. The validity of language and thought had been magnified and blown completely out of proportion, promoting, for most of us, what we believed was our reality. In generation after generation, the supposed experts informed us about what had merit and value, and what did not. No effective means other than language and verbal interaction could be cultivated and employed, or could it?

BABY STEPS

At first there were many discordant voices crying out the same message. We must unite! We must unite! Out of this rush to speak the new truth, a beautiful type of chaos arose. But, this would not do. Sensing this dilemma, interpreters came forward, ready to convey the new emergent truth to the many organizations around the world. Thus, began the initiative to produce what would ultimately become a global love convergence.

Resources were necessary to send envoys to all the corners of our world, seeking those who were adept and gifted in alternative methods of communication. Those whose hearts yearned for change, and who were in a position to make a difference, contributed mightily. Multitudes were standing by, ready to take action and participate in bringing about positive change, willing to do whatever was necessary to transform the quality of life. Through this commitment of the heart, a new vision began to crystallize.

THE SEARCH

In order to facilitate a major global shift, we would need an entirely new way to convey our thoughts. Within our collective consciousness, a handful of the wisest among us began to remember the way of the ancients. Underneath the incessant superficial chatter, bypassing the mental process of the mind, the original primordial way was rediscovered. Deep within, we possessed the innate gift of knowing from beyond the mentality of thought. This deep well of shared intuition had long since been ignored and forgotten.

Learning to depend on language had left us undeveloped, even as this ancient power was sleeping and dormant within us. With the passage of time, over centuries, even the awareness that we possessed this precious gift had all but slipped away.

Clearly this ability was exactly what would be needed to circumvent the language barrier entirely. Even more importantly, this ancient ability would be undetectable to the old ruling order.

Thus, it was decided that intuitive communication would become the primary means of interaction, transforming all manner of collaboration from that moment on.

Emissaries set out to seek those who were naturally gifted in non-verbal connectivity, and at first it was not known if this quest would be successful.

Indeed, it was a surprising reward to find that hidden among us, there existed many dedicated, talented individuals whose intuitive, psychic, and telepathic expertise was alive and well, fully activated, and performing effortlessly. These accomplished and brilliant souls were invited to join together at a central location.

This was ultimately written in our history as the most enlightened gathering of all time.

After attempting many personal and collective elucidations, still using numerous interpreters, we realized the enormity of what lay ahead. Yet, these crucial meetings bore sweet fruit, as an oath was sworn and a bond was forged by each one present.

In a courageous and ingenious undertaking, at last we had chosen one dramatic yet simplistic method of global transformation. Throughout the course of our planetary explorations, spread across our entire world, literally thousands of ley lines, song lines, sacred sites, and energetic crossing points had been discovered. These planetary geocenters had existed from time immemorial. Our plan was to connect intuitively through a unified focused projection of love. Harnessing the power of love, projected through our bonded intuition, we would connect to each other through these primal currents flowing around our entire world, generating an uplifting wave that could transform all life.

The goal was to create our own Centres, located as closely as possible to the natural sacred geo-energy sites that were emitting the planetary source energy into the atmosphere. We would design ways to integrate our emotional, intuitive, and psychic vision of one planet working together into the stream of energy being released through the geocenters and simultaneously connect across the face of our planet. Our hope was that, even though we were small in numbers, our collective strength of purpose would intensify exponentially when joined with the great global energy continuously encircling our planet. If we could ride this wave and connect through what would become our own newly constructed Centres, we could amplify and intensify our projected vision of love. This was our devoted quest, the dream we were dedicated to bringing to fruition.

Utilizing specific astronomical and astrological calculations, the most powerful times to unite were determined. These times and dates corresponded directly to our long-standing knowledge of the recurring influences of our surrounding planets and stars. When these celestial events occurred in the heavens, they could be instantaneously seen and known globally, giving us the ability to easily synchronize our actions.

While attending the first global gathering, the intuitives and empaths had become very close, remaining constantly connected. This continuity of communication further refined their mutual telepathy and visionary empathy, vastly enhancing their combined shared abilities. Consequently, information flowed freely through this group of individuals, even as they ultimately spread out across the great expanse. The celestial calendar of regional, national, and international events was then set to the hour, minute, and second of accuracy. Once completed, the assembled messengers returned to their home regions to communicate the plan. Upon arrival, they began transmitting and demonstrating the necessary techniques.

It must be noted that although most of our population was sympathetic, receptive, and even hopeful, the vast majority did not truly believe it was possible to realize such an achievement of this magnitude. Even we were not completely confident. These were immense undertakings that to many seemed truly impossible to coordinate.

The sheer magnitude of manifesting the energy of Focused Love Projection into existence requires absolute faith and a tremendous command of vision and emotional commitment. We were fortunate there was technology already spanning the globe that could transmit information instantaneously. Sending out the call, we brought together those who aligned in harmony with our goals and beliefs. They also commanded the technical genius to orchestrate these global actions. While these were difficult and seemingly overwhelming challenges, the spirit of bringing our dream to life was filled with breathtaking excitement.

Believing that this was the most important challenge anyone had yet endeavored to accomplish, everyone overflowed with exuberance and anticipation in pursuit of realizing our glorious vision of transformation.

THE LEAP

Our premiere planetary event was a tremendous achievement. From all of our established energy Centres which had been strategically positioned across the land, we were able to *simultaneously* focus, tuning into the sacred geo-sites emitting intense energy of planetary rejuvenation to organize an intuitive projection of the purest expression of love. This produced, at the exact coordinated instant, a harmonized global fusion. We were able to monitor the response through the input from the communication devices that had been placed around our world. The impact was astonishing. So much so, that as these results went out across the land, more and more participants longed to be a part of this magnificent work. We were triumphing beyond our greatest expectations!

Imagine the thrill of being present and seeing the birth of a new vision of life as it spread out across an entire planet. Intuitives and telepaths, psychics, indigenous shamans, and geo-sensitive energy workers, musicians, artists, and heart-centered healers were all drawn together in a singular unified soul intention. Multitudes gathered to share this deepest unity and experience and profound passions of the heart. Emerging from our world, these planetary gatherings were beautifully connected through powerful vortexes and crossing lines of energy forces. Our initial gatherings flowed forth to the world from these special energy Centres on waves of purest love.

The sight and sense of so many spirits in synchronous harmony streaming forth their love emanations forming a heart-to-heart connection and shining their light from each location was breathtaking. The geo-energy sites combined to further the flow, expanding and joining all the sites into one huge circuit of love. As the unifying consciousness of each site became fused into one grand expression of our highest qualities, all living beings were supercharged by its impact. The message of pure peace and world unity as a people was magnificent and inspired all it touched.

Although many spirit-filled enthusiasts flocked to the many Centres, our numbers still needed to grow. We required the kind of impact to influence essentially billions of our peoples and perhaps even trillions of life forms. This magnitude of bonding and unification would be necessary to accomplish the energetic, massive complete paradigm shift to break free from the old ways.

News of our endeavors spread to distant shores, but many sympathizers were unable to travel the great distances to be present at the power centers and add their heart energy to the ongoing expressions of focused love. Unknown to us at the time, as each scheduled energy event began, sympathetic champions of our movement, numbering in the millions, began projecting their support in silent rapport from wherever they were. Privately or in groups, they banded together and poured out their passionate energy, connecting through intuition and love. Each sacred geo-site bore its own uniqueness within the global love circuit and had a rare aspect of emotional texture associated with its specific energy signature. Many shining from afar felt a kindred spirit in their own heart to some or all of these sacred sites. Much to their amazement and surprise, an unexpected mutual reception arose. Their expression of love was mirrored back to them, and they experienced the most exquisite and extraordinary feeling of ultimate joy in return!

THE OLD AWAKENS

The many different government, economic, and political systems from around the world, which appeared to be separate, had all along been secretly linked together to form their global network of dominance. They began to take notice that something was changing, but they were baffled and unaware of the imminent shift that was underway.

It started to become alarmingly evident that fewer citizens were continuing to adhere to their rigid regime. Their supporters, who had historically cooperated in furthering their agenda, were no longer interfacing with them.

In giving the people the ability to peer behind the curtain, our whole population began to see the truth for the first time, and the insidious web of deceit that had unknowingly been skillfully woven around them.

After their eyes were opened, they began disengaging from The Order's materialistic agenda, as they finally understood the way it promoted jealousy, mistrust, competitiveness, and acquisition of personal possessions at all costs.

Having underestimated us, in utter disbelief, the controlling faction was shocked when they discovered that a global shift was happening. Credence had not previously been given to this so-called "movement," because the chronicle of their complete dominance had existed for millennia.

When those in positions of power finally woke up and realized a renaissance was underway, all methods of force and fear tactics were used to stop it. Unaware the expansive energy expression of our highest love was the transformative tool being used; no knowledge had been formulated to give instruction on how to disrupt our growing unity.

The inability to fathom the possibility that the power of the focused projection of love through unity in oneness could have such consequences greatly hindered their ability to enact a specific plan of defense. To our advantage, by the time the old order recognized the winds of change, many of us had thoroughly developed our ability to communicate without the use of spoken language. Further still, even this simple concept was beyond the boundaries of understanding to the ruling class. The emergence of the new vanguard continued to unite and sweep the globe as the rulers questioned their stability, and sheer panic prevailed.

Throughout their entire history, there was no record of this type of event, so they never developed a strategic plan of action to combat the uprising. Dumbfounded, they asked themselves, "How do we deal with a movement of this magnitude?" War was the answer.

Desperate attempts to intimidate us ensued as whole armies marched out to conquer and crush the new advancements. The regions where people lived in peace and love were targeted. Yet, by the virtue of our ability to instantaneously communicate intuitively, when they arrived, no one was there!

Over and over again, we escaped the arrival of the armies, which kept most of us safe. Sadly, many of the energy Centres were dismantled and destroyed, but thankfully, it was too late. Utilizing the powerful energy that had been attuned to the natural expressions of the planet, our connections had been strengthened and were complete, and surface structures were no longer necessary. Physical structures could be destroyed, but the energy emitting from the geocenters, imbued and amplified by countless heart connections, could not.

A slow exodus began, as pilgrimages from the most populated areas of our planet brought us to new locations to start over. New villages, which grew into hamlets, towns, and cities, began to spring up in areas that had previously been unpopulated. We were learning to live in cooperation and harmony, dedicated to love. Our emergence of compassion ushered in a synergistic collaboration, leading to completely new ways of living.

New methods to fulfill the needs of the entire planet's population came into existence, bringing about prosperity and abundance for all.

Finally, the ruling elite began to understand the simple, but unstoppable truth in unity that our world was now embracing. Hoping to confuse and fool the masses, they advanced new leaders who blatantly plagiarized the new slogans of love of humanity and benefit for all. Attempting to disguise their new plan, they made it appear on the surface to be almost the same as our own, but it was really only a set of diversions and distractions designed to lead us back to the controlling systems of the past.

Lacking the necessary selflessness, authentic caring, and loving heart to awaken, they were totally disconnected from our new way of life. They didn't possess the awareness to tap into what was occurring, as our expanded consciousness was beyond their comprehension. It was impossible for them to access the ability to communicate intuitively.

They were only interested in profit, greed, and division, and there was no place for them in the new land. Witnessing their entire known history being dismantled caused a flood of hysteria in those whose main concern was acquisition and power.

More and more people were defecting, as huge sections of society deserted long-standing centers of propaganda and indoctrination. The masses began to experience the exhilaration of love through the wave of new energy flowing across the planet. For a while, our society was in chaos and deep turmoil as the greedy ones tried every means possible to remain in power. But we could not be swayed, because the shouting of their empty spoken words was silenced, paling in the face of our intuitive communication, which was far beyond mere language.

Every deception was attempted. Mass amounts of so-called "luxury items" were given away for free, as they tried desperately to keep the people engaged and distracted, so they could be drawn back to the old ways. When this didn't work, clandestine campaigns were engaged, utilizing the strategy of false flags. Terrorist acts were perpetrated, as those in power tried to shift the blame for these outrageous deeds onto us. The deceptions they attempted to use in their struggle to lure the population back to the ways of the past simply did not work.

We had expanded far beyond that type of communication, but they still could not grasp how failure befell them at every turn. There was no going back, once the pure joy and contentment of being connected to the all-encompassing emergence of love was experienced by the people! *Truly, this proved to be their downfall.*

Even though large portions of the communication systems around our planet were eventually disrupted and destroyed, we could not be stopped.

This tactic had been anticipated. By utilizing previously prepared star charts, we continued to facilitate the intricate timing of our events, intuitively promoting the ongoing spontaneous participation of all inhabitants, from all geographic locations. Our enduring projection of love shone forth in all directions with ever-expanding intensity. The energy forces, geocenters, and vortexes we established were completely invisible to them.

Our numbers grew, as the vast majority of cultures began feeling the exhilarating energy of the movement. When the soldiers and armies began to feel what was really happening, they instantly awoke and collectively refused to fight any longer. Their weapons just fell from their hands. *Without the control of force, the selfish masters could no longer maintain dominance.* It became evident that their plot to regain control was devolving, and in a relatively short amount of time the old agenda was relegated to the status of an unhealthy social virus. Still, the old order marched on, continuing their fight and wreaking havoc until their final breath.

Once the epitome of power, these would-be masters were reduced to smaller and smaller factions, soon becoming pathetic social pariahs slinking off into the shadows. Destroyed by their own hand, the rigid forces of their own making simply collapsed under the weight of its own obsolescence.

The most compelling mission of our movement was to render the mental process of spoken language extinct. By abolishing this method of control, countless millennia of suffering and enslavement had been vanquished.

Once we had risen above these methods and communicated directly through our hearts and intuition, the outmoded form of verbal communication quickly became less and less effective. It was finally seen for what it was, merely a device; a tool that had blinded us in a cloud of deception.

This dark sordid chapter of our early history finally came to a close. *Lifting the veil from our eyes, dispelling the mists of our minds, we finally saw The Light and remembered the truth of our authentic loving nature.*

VICTORY

With the advent of the old guard fading from influence, doubts that might have existed in the hearts and minds of anyone who watched or engaged in these events were dissolved.

The planetary population soon realized the territorial lines dividing them had been merely fabricated attempts to forge false separation and division, dictated through history by kings and tyrants, dictators, and, yes, even crusaders. Clearly seen as nonexistent, these invisible boundaries were exposed for the chains they were. Through this glorious revelation, the far-off lands of our world united as One.

When love, the most powerful connecting force in all Creation, joined the hearts and minds of those living on our planet in a unified bond, miraculous possibilities manifested. Not only had we fulfilled our mission, we had exceeded beyond our wildest expectations.

At last, we could sing out in great celebration of our transformational breakthrough into freedom. Souls who had become conduits of Light, through which the consciousness of love, intuition telepathy, and empathy had shined, joined with the vast sea of extraordinarily gifted coordinators and facilitators. Everyone embraced the new horizon of enlightenment.

These beacons of the new age never imagined they would be named the originators and pioneers of what would one day be celebrated as one of the grandest events of our history. Looking back into this epoch of deep conflict and great transformation, it is easy to see that without these brave souls and their courageous quest for spiritual freedom, the ability to traverse the boundless gulf of evolution, might never have come to be!

These were the earliest and first venues the new heralds utilized to enlighten and uplift all the living beings of our world. We were able to switch into a new state of unity through an awareness of consciousness that no one thought possible. Those who witnessed the profound journey and destined arrival of those early souls, truly believe it was the rediscovery and refinement of elevated intuitive communication that transcended the old spoken language. More than any other achievement, this one major development precipitated our great leap forward.

Growing exponentially as a people in a relatively short time, we began a new way of interacting with higher consciousness. Through the evolutionary children of divine birth, new fountains of truth flowed into existence. Amazing, brilliant, extraordinary Beings were born in wave after wave, possessing talents and abilities far greater than any that came before. Moving onward, our spiritual awakening continued to flourish as each generation brought forth exceptional new gifts.

Totally awake and fully developed by adolescence, we reverently welcomed these new advanced souls as the radiant hearts and brightest spirit lights that had ever shown on our world.

Over time, the old ways withered, turned to dust, and soon became a distant memory. Dancing to the music of a new day, it seemed like our new song of life would play on forever.

THE NEW DAWN

Initially, it was not immediately clear to us, and little did we know, that we were planting a new seed of awakening into our collective consciousness.

Our evolution as a people blossomed out of the sheer joy of our innate ability to love and be loved unconditionally. Elevated awareness connected our hearts and minds, which grew and became like a neural net.

Far in advance of anything we formerly conceived, we became the generators of a collective genius through the unification of this initial first, or original, global fusing. A worldwide organic consciousness grew that any former technologies could only pale before.

Hunger, homelessness, and oppression no longer existed. We began to breathe again, as millennia of fear were released. Flourishing in the new fresh air, many of us became creative contributors, joyfully seeing to the task of fulfilling the needs of all life.

Freed from controlling restraints, science and technology harnessed new resources and created monumental breakthroughs that further enriched the quality of life's atmosphere around the world.

Receiving long-awaited support and acknowledgment, the futurists among us were ready to enact their plans to brilliantly restructure our day-to-day lives for the totality of society, and they were wholeheartedly encouraged to proceed.

Soon, extraordinary, meaningful, and abundant lifestyles, once out of reach for most, became available to everyone through the confluence of like minds and hearts. Our people were happy, healthy, and abundant through expansive ongoing innovations designed and implemented for the betterment of all.

Projected love energy spread across the land, much like living waters, overflowing and rushing out toward all horizons. The instant these waves connected, the radiance of one integrated circuit of love surrounded our planet.

The law of emergence was the key that unlocked our ability to reach this glorious pinnacle. The soul-seed of our origins had blossomed magnificently as we basked in the sun of our full potential, proclaiming our destiny fulfilled.

Many cycles of the moon and stars passed, as personal empowerment and soul freedom emanated from and through each and every life. Our new collective life became a celebration of unity, bestowed upon us by the flowering of the Light!

There were often times along our way when we would reach a time of great abundance and harmony. It was during these periods when we felt as though this was it, we had made it, as there certainly couldn't be anything greater than what we had achieved. Coming to see the naiveite of these perceptions would dawn when the next symbol or sign of what was yet to come would make itself known.

THE PLANET GLOWS

The portent of our next step was nothing less than miraculous. Seemingly all at once, high above, we began to see energy streams emerging from the sacred planetary geo-sites. Arcing across our skies, glorious beams of light spanning huge distances blazed into view.

These interwoven bands of colorized energy were like an iridescent rainbow becoming denser and brighter, covering our entire world.

The skies continued to shine brighter and brighter, until our entire planet began to glow. Transfixed and suspended in the rapture of this awe-inspiring moment we witnessed the power of these incomparable intertwining planetary light waves arc out across our entire world. Imagine the heightened sense of joy and bliss welling up within us, as the Light of our whole world continued expanding, revealing greater and greater realities of energy transformation.

Rising from deep within the core of our planet, we heard and sensed the very force of gravity resonating outward in all directions. Like soft low voices, mysterious at first, each of us felt our hearts and minds being re-tuned to a new frequency. Barely audible yet continuing to grow, this resonance arose in a concentration of combined intensity radiating through all life.

This expanding vibration of our inner planetary gravitation continued reaching upward, and connected to the frequencies of the orbiting arcs of light. Suddenly, in a revelation of clarity, the essential truth was revealed. At last, we realized what was happening. Our collective destinies were being joined in rapturous realignment with the surrounding cosmos.

Ringing out strong and clear the new sound was the combined reverberation of all peoples, and the planet itself, rising up to the heavens as One voice, One sound, One vibration, and One all-encompassing love. Our whole world in complete unity had taken on a new and unique mantle!

THE SHIFT

Playing on and on, our collective soul song became the majestic sound of our entire world. We could feel the gravitational force rising from the center of our planet, flowing up through the soles of our feet and ascending out through the tops of our heads.

Illuminating the space around us unlike any experience before, the waves of gravity became visible, permeating every particle of our essence as they illuminated the textures and fabric of the many dimensions surrounding us.

A transformation was taking place, physically changing our planet and us. *The infusion of light was lessening our physical density and advancing the expansion of our consciousness and comprehension.* With each transformation, as we were impacted by infinite gravity our changing essence produced a brand new song with a unique vibration all its own.

Only when a planet is ready to make its ascension, having completed its journey of nurturing the life that was placed in its care, can a gravitational frequency shift like this occur.

Reaching this new level of perception, it was clearly visible how all creation is held in the finest detail of individuation and meticulously maintains its authenticity.

Gravitation permeates all dimensions and, like love, is a supreme force without which reality could not exist.

The rarity of this type of event is indescribable. Every living creation that has been lovingly cherished and developed under the care of the great Being that nurtures this world must also be sufficiently evolved to take the next evolutionary leap. A shift of this magnitude can only occur when both are in perfect synchronicity, ready to burst forward in one simultaneous transformation.

We had evolved as a species and become an integral part of a spectacular and extraordinary moment. This celestial event, unparalleled in its magnificence, would forever be celebrated and honored as a wondrous new beginning, the sacred moment of our grand emergence.

The combined spontaneous and synchronistic evolution of a planet and its people reaching out toward its creator in one brilliant blaze of love flashed across the galaxy! *We became the rarest of celestial jewels, a super nova of consciousness.*

Instantaneously came the momentous broadcast announcing our arrival into the new cosmic community. The moment our soul awakened, the reality of our fulfillment and attainment as a planet and a people went out across a multitude of star systems, reaching toward Source itself.

As the totality of all life and the planet converged and merged in this spectacular evolutionary shift, we were elevated into a new, more expanded dimension that emitted light and sound so beautiful it could be seen and felt throughout all known and unknown realities.

In days of old, when farmers carefully prepared their soil and planted each seed, a prayer was offered in the hope that each seed would reach its full growth and flower abundantly. Then the farmer would wait patiently, hoping the seed would grow and one day spiral through the top of the ground seeking the light. This was always a day of great rejoicing, as the farmer reaped the reward of his efforts and gave thanks, knowing that his prayers had been answered. It was a grand day worthy of the greatest of celebrations, when each seedling turned its face to the sun!

So too, was this glorious moment for us.

Like seedlings, we had broken through to reach our divine birthright and spiraled up in rapture, turning our collective vision toward the one truth of all.

This most assuredly was one of the greatest single bursts forward our world would ever experience. A quantum leap had occurred. We would now move away from the slow grinding process of our former development, and into a new elevated evolution of life.

As we became more and more radiant, this moment brought spherical dimensions into sight, which had been invisible to us until now. We perceived clearly the parallel evolutionary timelines that had always existed, but our sleeping eyes had not been able to fully see them through our unknowing hearts.

Love fused gravitation enabled our vision to literally

fold back the fabric of an infinitude of different dimensions. Unique otherworldly Beings were revealed through our elevated consciousness. Beings who were born to these delicate sources of life had been woven, like us, into the finest of life-creations, and we were all evolving along the grand way.

Having completed their own rites of passage, voices rang out in celebration from the many worlds surrounding ours. *The music of joy from these worlds honored our spiritual rebirth.* Celebrations from beyond our planetary shores filled our senses and we knew we were not alone.

At this very moment, emanating in a thoroughly inexplicable way, gleaming starships, mystical vessels, and other vehicles of time transport etherealized in the starscape surrounding our world. Apparently they had been there all along but had been unknown to us until now. Their appearance further expanded our vision demonstrating the great possibilities of life that existed throughout the entire cosmos.

In one glorious chorus, a message rang out to each and every member of our race. It was a message that sounded within the heart of all the peoples of our world. This message was not one of thought, but rather it was one of love. Each of us heard the call, individually and universally, and it was felt by all who were present in this extraordinary moment of unique evolution, welcoming us home!

CONTACT

"Greetings beloved ones. On this magnificent occasion we come bearing glad tidings of great joy to commemorate the genesis of your transcendence. We have watched your struggles through the extraordinary journey of your heart's desire to embrace the love of all life. As the bringers of a new expression of love, we bear witness to the truth of your next sacred step into the Light."

In this moment vast multitudes of angelic presence, resplendent shining, showed themselves. Joining in this universal celebration, we could see that they too were flourishing along their own scheme of divine enlightenment. These were Celestial Beings, here to rejoice in our arrival and bear witness to our new relationship with Source. Their gift of radiant bliss flowed through us like a song from the heavens in ways beyond our comprehension.

How can I convey to you the overwhelming joy of receiving the outpouring of celestial radiance through this visible angelic presence? *It is simply indescribable.* Close your eyes and feel the exquisite splendor within you now. Imagine this glorious sensation expanded by infinity, and still it will be but a whisper of this sublime ecstasy.

Our people had always sought to embrace what we thought was the highest and most profound expression of love, never knowing how limited our conception of love was. Now, through these visitations, we were able to see and feel a never-ending realm of expanding love we never knew existed.

To celebrate our advancement, the visitors also brought symbolic torches of spirit fire that represented even higher concepts, visions and awareness of love. These felt like moments in which the gods themselves had come to us.

Although they seemed god-like, we knew they were not. They were, like us, the evolutionary sons and daughters of time and no-time.

Their appearance on our planet was an incomparable acknowledgment from the emissaries of our new cosmic family. They came to show us that Creation is brimming with countless forms of life and we are part of it.

Striving with all of our might to gather ourselves into oneness, we had paid little attention to our place in the universe. Now, in an exclamation of joy, we realized there were trillions upon trillions of other Beings and countless other worlds witnessing and observing our ongoing development. By virtue of our attainment and new ability to communicate through focused projected love, at last the time had come. Without realizing it, we had discovered and greatly developed psychic telepathy, the wordless language of all advanced Beings. Communication with this vast range of life was now possible.

Through our heightened and embellished vision, we were able to see the inconceivable breadth of life that inhabited previously unknown worlds, existing throughout Creation both near and beyond.

There were evolutionary life designs similar to ourselves, as well as new unique Beings entirely unfamiliar to us. Some were evolving dimensional life designs, making their way through space and time. Others seemed to be celestial creations that were not part of time development at all!

HOMECOMING

Angelic, cosmic, divine, and many other fantastic forms of evolutionary life had been revealed to us, along with Beings who looked almost exactly like us! Imagine what a surprise it was when we realized the extraordinary truth. *These Beings actually were us!*

Having inhabited our planet many cycles past, they had evolved into their own moment of transformation. In doing so, they were able to rise up off our planet, and through dimensional travel explore the infinite wonders of the universe.

Now, on the currents of universal gravity transcending our limited concepts of time, our own brothers and sisters had returned home to us. Their arrival here in this moment was a triumphant exclamation of deep joy-filled pride that we had also found our way.

We had chosen to merge our collective minds and hearts in harmony with our planet to ultimately align and shift into our own divine destiny.

As they descended to walk among us and share their wisdom, we felt the connection of great bonding love.

It was then we truly realized and understood they *were* our extended family. Having dwelled on this planet eons ago, our brothers and sisters had long since freed themselves and ventured out to experience the mysteries of the unknown eternal regions of the Grand Creation. Continued evolution had afforded them the mastery of time and space, bestowing the ability to travel almost anywhere. They chose to return at this exact moment of our glorious awakening with beaming hearts, to nurture and inspire us as we embraced our new destiny. Many of these star travelers chose to stay with us for a time, enjoying the warm glow of a wondrous homecoming and celebration. Some of our people also accepted the invitation to join them, and continue on to experience the next wave of their cosmic journey.

We had stepped into the light of our consummate soul adventure. Those who long ago had already embraced the many paths of limitless diversity greeted us with boundless love. Welcomed with open hearts into the expansive community of life teeming all around us, we too would be able to ascend to infinite realms on high, never more to be alone.

This was a collective elevation into a new dimension, an amazing moment we wholeheartedly embraced. *We realized that, just as those who came before us, we too are rippling waves of creation. And the ripples will continue to flow on into eternity.* In absolute majesty, we beheld the awakened vision of Creation's never-ending cycle.

Presently, the moment to move forward was upon us. We welcomed those who were remaining as our own, and bid farewell to those who were departing. Angelic,

Celestial, and Divine Beings from every dimension, along with those expanded lives beyond time and space, lent their hearts to this celebration of soul enlightenment. Then and there, in that ultimate timeless moment we felt the loving embrace of all awakening life receiving us. Spirit evolution had opened the door and we walked straight through it into the open arms of our awaiting cosmic family!

Ablaze in a moment of unparalleled brilliance as we continued on our sacred journey, the bond we forged promised we would always be one, united with each beat of our hearts. The heavens burst alive in song and dancing resonance of the Light. The transcendent melodies that raised us remained and continued in unforgettable streams of flowing brilliance. Never again would our world be shrouded in darkness.

The moment was filled with absolute joy, as from every part of our world there came the voices of each heart joining in the celestial declaration of love in the highest. Our planet was immersed in a golden aura, and even from the farthest reaches of space came the voices of all creation ringing clear and true, proclaiming our acceptance. We were home and we had been born anew!

RETURN TO THE MOMENT

Yes! Those were extraordinary times.

The first beginnings of a new Source creation had unfolded, through the elevated expression of the law of emergence. As the old life fell away, a new seed had been planted and was seeking its perfection. This time we knew we were the seed and possessed the consciousness to grow in its presence.

All the Beings you see here in our City of Light are the descendants of those times. We are the living proof that through love, an upward turn away from the old and into a new evolutionary spiral can change the course of destiny for an entire people.

In our original biological expressions of life, we existed seemingly motionless for thousands of millennia. Ours was a painstakingly sluggish state of evolution. Yet, all I have shared of our emergence, from our deep barbaric beginnings to the super nova of consciousness, broadcasting the genesis of our gravitational frequency shift, and our subsequent arrival into the heart of our cosmic family, happened in less than a single age. It was a mere twinkling of Time's Eye. These transformational leaps, although extremely rare, are attributed completely and totally to the vision and efforts that ultimately led to the planetary convergence of those early pioneers. Through their efforts, fusing and merging the nature of love and essence into one collectively awakening life, they were able to turn our species away from our former dull and plodding existence. Because of their visionary transcendence, our shift into a new and grander destiny led us to an elevated awareness and embrace of all that flows from Source.

* * *

We were overwhelmed with wonder as we listened to our guide.

"We are totally astounded by your amazing odyssey. You have come such a long way from your early beginnings."

Our guide thanked us for our appreciation of all we had been shown, and we asked, "We were wondering. Has your city always been named Trasara?"

"Oh no," he said. "If we were to peer into the distant past, our world had many names, the last of which I believe was, EARTH…!"

"Earth. Why that's our…."

He smiles and, in an instant, he is gone.

We smile too, realizing the wonder that ultimately awaits.

FINAL WORDS

The warmth of Earth's glow greets us as we return to the familiar bodies we left at the beginning of our journey. Our world seems so very small after the exalted awe-inspiring realms of our travels, yet it is from here, in this very moment, we will always continue to rise.

Moving forward into our lives now, walking among the people of our lush green world, we beam brightly and continue to shine, radiating our light in all directions. Our inner light expresses a brilliant emanation, touching each and every soul, indeed, every living creation.

Some receive this illumination in conscious joy; others go about their lives completely unaware.

Nothing can stop the crest of love as it transforms all life on its journey through the heart of the universe. By learning to ride the Rippling Waves, perhaps we can create our own unique City of Light, or write an even greater, more glorious chapter of our destiny.

Clearly, we are not a sleepy ship gliding slowly through the fog, as we were once taught to believe. A new transformation can be achieved, without waiting an eternity for the break of dawn. We are swiftly awakening, and when morning manifests fully there will be those brave ones to come with gentle hand to shake us from our slumber—those who have viewed the first light in heartfelt compassion and rushed to tell of its splendor.

Our journey, although consummated, will continue ever onward.

The inherent desire within will forever call us, and the magic swirl of life will sweep us into its glow, delivering us to distant shores. Our story will unfold and be told in ways yet to be revealed.

Then, as the golden clouds of a new day reflect the radiant rays of the sun, we will dissolve into the waiting ocean of consciousness, reaching out to our ever-expanding destiny. Flowing on now, riding the crest of Rippling Waves into a never-ending eternity, with love in our hearts, we too, send forth glad tidings of joy.

ABOUT THE AUTHOR

As a child, Anthony began having unexplained visions of things yet to be, and a prescient knowing far beyond his years. Thankfully, being raised in a progressive family, his natural visionary abilities were supported and encouraged, giving them the space to flower and grow. He later discovered that he was the fourth generation in his family to be blessed with perceptions and visions, and as he matured into an adult, his desire to fully embrace these extraordinary gifts continued to grow.

Today, Anthony is a renowned clairvoyant, master astrologer, psychic visionary, sound healer and empath, highly respected for his compassion and integrity. Ever striving to grow into complete alignment with the highest states of consciousness, his soul mission has been the development, refinement, exploration and mastery of his intuitive and psychic nature.

An unquenchable thirst to know led to extensive study and a lifetime of experience, through which Anthony has attained a remarkable capacity to access and embody the worlds of vibrational healing, clairvoyance, psychic phenomenon, metaphysics, cosmology, mysticism, theosophy, ontology, eastern and western philosophy, Gnosticism, flower of life physics, psychology and beyond. Through the attainment of this vast knowledge, his passionate desire to realize full self-discovery and enlightened transformation grew, leading him to even more esoteric studies.

Following another soul-guided path, his spirit experienced the transformative healing force of sound, which drew him into the world of music and rhythmic expression. Years of complete dedication and unwavering discipline gave him total command over his instruments and inexplicable joy. Through this inner bliss, he was able to let go and fly, freeing himself from the restrictions of all the techniques learned, becoming a soaring vehicle for divine inspiration to flow through with spontaneous improvisation and effortless creativity. From these heights, new inspiration called to him, guiding him to design and create original and unique instruments of glorious sound and vibrational healing. This was a time of profound growth and fulfillment.

Longing to go even deeper, he gained further spiritual insight through the practice of single point meditation, which revealed a new sensory gift, the ability to communicate directly to consciousness through an unspoken language of the heart. Upon the activation of this heightened awakening, he began hearing and feeling the voices of those in need on a global scale, and felt compelled to rise to that call, for now was the time to share these gifts in a greater way. Anthony's true path was grounded in commitment and service to humanity. The totality of these experiences had become greater than the sum of their parts, and a new consolidated vehicle of expression emerged, compelling him to reach out as a beacon of understanding and hope, helping humanity and all those seeking a deeper truth to find and follow their own path of light.

Multifaceted eclectic pursuits continually opened his eyes to explore modern scientific fields, studies of celestial mechanics and quantum physics, along with religious and faith-based teachings and the mysterious ancient writings that held the wisdom of civilizations long past. Upon many years of soul reflection, he came to finally see that *all* of these expressions of creation are truly one and the same.

Recently, Anthony has passionately studied the emerging fields of neural plasticity, epigenetics, heart-mind coherence and the wondrous concepts relating to *The Field*. The blossoming of Anthony's natural born gifts bore the unique capacity to tune in to the realm of universal knowledge and the hidden mysteries of the cosmos. This knowing empowers him to see, hear and, most importantly, interpret messages from spirit, revealing profound inner truths. This revelation was made possible as he has been granted passage through multidimensional portals of consciousness that link humanity with the realm of infinite possibility, both here in this plain of existence and beyond.

Choosing to travel the path of the mystic visionary, Anthony's journey simultaneously flowed into cosmic attunement, musical revelations, multifaceted creativity and artistic expression.

Bridging both the physical and celestial forces giving him a pure connection with the realms of the cosmic and divine, his expanded perceptive sensitivity is intimately attuned to a chorus of heavenly guides and the infinite eternal beings that watch over us all. Born with expanded awareness, Anthony has always been touched by and connected with the divine presence that surrounds and flows through every living creation. This is a precious blessing that has given him untold insight into the limitless nature of Being.

Anthony is a multidimensional traveler who fuses his innate gifts with intelligence and the wisdom born of heart-centered intuition. He has taught and administered spiritual healing and guidance to thousands of people around the globe as they search to experience and understand the unseen forces that shape and transform all of our lives.

Universal love is the deepest truth, and that love is the Source of all existence. Anthony's heartfelt quest is to continue spreading this simple yet all-encompassing truth throughout the world.

To learn more or to contact Anthony Teresi, please visit https://Anthonyteresi.com.

A GLOBAL LOVE AFFAIR

A Global Love Affair is a humanitarian organization founded by Anthony Teresi. It is dedicated to uplifting the quality of life and the unification of all the inhabitants of our planet. The mission of A Global Love Affair is to bypass the mind and the purely mental constructs of that false reality, and utilize intuition and the expression of love. Focusing these qualities through the power centers of our planet, we will create a quantum shift of connectivity across all of the barriers that currently divide us. This will be the first known circuit of planetary love utilizing the resources of our world for the betterment of all.

As is illustrated in *Rippling Waves,* we are shown the ultimate future of humanity and all life on our planet by achieving this end. Through reaching the highest states of awareness to facilitate a quickening of consciousness, the destiny of the human race can change. *Through love, a shift in our awareness can find its way into an accelerated evolution.*

As human beings inhabiting earth, we are empowered to bridge the current global crisis point and move on to this end. A Global Love Affair is a well-planned approach that projects a planetary scope of action unlike any we have seen. It brings into being the one common force of unity we all possess: our mutual heart connection. *Love is the way to the quantum shift, the Ascension so often spoken of these days.* Yet, little has been done to enact these principles.

With the recent breakthroughs in physics, coinciding with the reemergence of ancient wisdom at our disposal, we have it within our grasp to shift the energy of the entire planet to a higher frequency. Long thought to be impossible, the recent convergence of new and ancient truth marks the path. The planetary movement as outlined by A Global Love Affair demonstrates the logistics of this endeavor. We realize that this is a bold statement and an even bolder move, alluding to the ability that we can unite an entire planet. Yet, in truth, the vision stands before us, simply awaiting our enactment.

If we join within the unity of universal love's connection, we will prevail in taking all of humanity to its highest potential. *We can build a new model. This can happen.* Creating a global circuit of love is the answer, and many organizations already exist that are dedicated to this purpose. The technology also exists to facilitate the coordination of global events designed to create these realities. There is almost no place on the planet that is not technologically connected. A Global Love Affair calls on all of the organizations, as well as all of the adepts in the master art of intuition, to join and rise above the current levels of confusion, chaos, and deliberate misdirection and elevate our shared humanistic goals into a new reality.

For a more comprehensive look at what we propose, please watch the introduction to this movement entitled *Earth's Chakras* on our website or on the YouTube link below.

Earth's Chakras

https://www.youtube.com/watch?v=rV1v8REvXAg

The Call

*A poem of first realizations by
Anthony Teresi*

I know now 'tis messengers we are,
Dawned to help others fly fast and far.

I can see it coming through us and on to them.
I can see us rising again and again.

Over and over together we'll soar
Until Oneness becomes a deafening roar.

Then with the greatest sweep of our might
We'll joyously rise and melt into light.

'Tis then we'll know the parts are whole
And there really isn't any "place" to go.

Then when from All returned to I,
It's to help teach the next ones to fly.

Over and over the journey is made,
Showing the way, showing the way.

It's now I realize, it's now I see.
Allow me please, this privilege to be.

www.ingramcontent.com/pod-product-compliance
Lightning Source LLC
Chambersburg PA
CBHW071810080526
44589CB00012B/737